SHIR HASHIRIM

A MODERN COMMENTARY
ON THE SONG OF SONGS

Translation and commentary by
LEONARD S. KRAVITZ
and
KERRY M. OLITZKY

URJ PRESS
NEW YORK, NEW YORK

Library of Congress Cataloging-in-Publication Data

Kravitz, Leonard S.
    Shir hashirim : a modern commentary on the Song of songs/Leonard S. Kravitz
and Kerry M. Olitzky.
        p. cm.
    Includes the text of the Song of Solomon in Hebrew and English.
    ISBN 0-8074-0896-4 (pbk. : alk. paper)
    1. Bible. O.T. Song of Solomon—Commentaries.   I. Olitzky, Kerry M.
II. Bible. O.T. Song of Solomon. Hebrew. 2003.   III. Bible. O.T. Song of Solomon. English.
Kravitz-Olitzky. 2003. IV. Title.

BS1485.53 .K73 2003
223'.9077—dc21

                                                                    2002032228

Typesetting: El Ot Ltd., Tel Aviv
This book is printed on acid-free paper.
Copyright © 2004 by URJ Press
Manufactured in the United States of America
10 9 8 7 6 5 4 3 2 1

For Hanna,
for everything.
LSK

For Sheryl,
on our twenty-fifth wedding anniversary.
KMO

Permissions

Every attempt has been made, where necessary, to obtain permission to reprint previously published material. The authors gratefully acknowledge the following for permission to reprint previously published material:

CCAR: Excerpt from *Yearbook of the Central Conference of American Rabbis,* vol. 101–2, 1991–1992. Reprinted by permission of the Central Conference of American Rabbis.

AMY EILBERG: Excerpt "Hol Hamo-ed Pesach: Seeking Rebirth, Intimacy," by Amy Eilberg from *Jewish Bulletin of Northern California,* April 2, 1999. Copyright © 1999 by Rabbi Amy Eilberg. Permission granted by Rabbi Amy Eilberg.

FARRAR, STRAUS AND GIROUX: Excerpt from *A Time for Every Purpose Under Heaven* by Arthur Ocean Waskow and Phyllis Ocean Berman. Copyright © 2002 by Arthur Ocean Waskow and Phyllis Ocean Berman. Reprinted by permission of Farrar, Straus and Giroux, LLC.

MICHAEL GOLD: Excerpt from *The Ten Journeys of Life: Walking the Path of Abraham* by Michael Gold. Copyright © 2001 by Rabbi Michael Gold. Permission granted by Rabbi Michael Gold.

JASON ARONSON: Excerpt from *Judaism on Pleasure* by Reuven Bulka. Reprinted by permission of Jason Aronson; excerpt from *Paradigm Shift: From the Jewish Renewal Teachings of Reb Zalman Schachter-Shalomi* edited by Ellen Singer. Reprinted by permission of Jason Aronson; excerpt from *God, Love, Sex and Family: A Rabbi's Guide for Building Relationships that Last* by Michael Gold. Reprinted by permission of Jason Aronson.

JEWISH LIGHTS: Excerpt from *These Are the Words: A Vocabulary of Jewish Spiritual Life* © 2000 Arthur Green (Woodstock, VT: Jewish Lights Publishing). $18.95+$3.75 s/h; excerpt from *Sacred Intentions* © 1999 Rabbi Kerry M. Olitzky and Rabbi Lori Forman

(Woodstock, VT: Jewish Lights Publishing). $15.95 + $3.75 s/h; excerpt from *ReVisions: Seeing Torah Through a Feminist Lens* © 1998 by Rabbi Elyse Goldstein (Woodstock, VT: Jewish Lights Publishing). $19.95 + $3.75 s/h; excerpt from *Eyes Remade for Wonder: A Lawrence Kushner Reader* © 1998 by Lawrence Kushner (Woodstock, VT: Jewish Lights Publishing). $18.95 + $3.75 s/h; and excerpt from *Self, Struggle and Change: Family Conflict Stories in Genesis and Their Healing Insights for Our Lives* © 1995 Norman J. Cohen (Woodstock, VT: Jewish Lights Publishing). $19.95 + $3.75 s/h. Order by mail or call 800-962-4544 or online at www.jewishlights.com. Permission granted by Jewish Lights Publishing, P.O. Box 237, Woodstock, VT 05091.

THE JEWISH PUBLICATION SOCIETY: Reprinted from *The Jewish Moral Virtues,* by Eugene Borowitz, © 1999, published by The Jewish Publication Society with the permission of the publisher, The Jewish Publication Society.

KTAV: Excerpt from "Jewish Spirituality: The Way of Love" by Carol Ochs in *Paths of Faithfulness: Personal Essays on Jewish Spirituality* edited by Carol Ochs, Kerry M. Olitzky, and Joshua Saltzman. Reprinted by permission of KTAV.

JANET MARDER: excerpt from "Climbing Jacob's Ladder: Jewish Teachings on the Messiah" by Janet Marder from Sermon Archives December 15, 2000. Reprinted by permission of Rabbi Janet Marder.

PENGUIN GROUP: From *The Busy Soul* by Terry Bookman, copyright © 1999 by Rabbi Terry Bookman. Used by permission of Perigee Books, an imprint of Penguin Group (USA) Inc.

MELINDA RIBNER: Excerpt from New Age Judaism: Ancient Wisdom for the Modern World by Melinda Ribner. Reprinted by permission of Melinda Ribner.

TORAH AURA PRODUCTIONS: Excerpt from *Building Jewish life: Passover Activity Book* by Joel Lurie Grishaver. Reprinted by permission of Torah Aura Productions.

Contents

Acknowledgments

More than the various other projects we have undertaken together, this book has truly been a labor of love, for the text reflects the love of man and woman, of God and human, and of two friends who share a passion for Judaism and the sacred text. And as we continued to learn from the text and its commentaries, we similarly learned from each other—something that has drawn us together as colleagues and friends for nearly twenty years.

We would like to thank our friends at the URJ Press, particularly its editor Rabbi Hara Person, who has nurtured us and guided this project and others along the way. We add to that thanks also to Ken Gesser, Liane Broido, Lauren Dubin, Rabbi Annie Belford, and Michael Goldberg. We acknowledge the leadership of Rabbi Eric Yoffie, who has made a return to the primary sources a priority of his tenure as president of the Union for Reform Judaism, an effort we applaud and heartily endorse. And we also recognize with appreciation the work of Rabbi David Ellenson, who, as president of Hebrew Union College–Jewish Institute of Religion, has renewed the dialogue between Jewish tradition and modernity.

We thank colleagues, students, and friends at Hebrew Union College–Jewish Institute of Religion and the Jewish Outreach Institute. They have privileged us with the opportunity to live and work among those whose "occupation is Torah," and we feel extremely blessed as a result. Finally and most importantly, we express our profound gratitude to our families, who constantly support our insatiable thirst for the redemptive waters of Torah.

Leonard S. Kravitz
Kerry ("Shia") Olitzky
Tu BiSh'vat 5762

Introduction

The Song of Songs, known in Hebrew as *Shir HaShirim,* gained importance as a sacred text because of its various interpretations rather than because of its plain meaning. The book is a collection of erotic love poetry whose sexual images are somewhat softened only by the amount of time that has passed between the compilation of the book and our day. It is a dialogue between two lovers that is marked by love songs, poetic dialogues, and monologues. Some just call it a love poem—or a series of love poems—that champions the physical expression of that love. The lovers who are the main characters in this book express their physical yearnings in frank terms and graphic sexual images, even as they communicate their more profound and enduring love for one another. Their love deepens their appreciation for the beautiful landscape that provides a context for their relationship and is, as well, exquisitely described. As a result, some of the most exceptional poetry in the Bible is contained in the Song of Songs. The transformation from love poetry to Holy Scripture (*Kitvei HaKodesh*) reflects both cultural development and a concomitant shifting of values.

Since the book was embedded in folk religion, it had to be raised to a more spiritual level before it could enter the biblical canon, especially when it is later interpreted by the Rabbis. Whatever the poem meant originally, it came to mean something very different as time passed. As a result, it was not the meaning in the text that entranced succeeding generations of its readers but the meaning that was brought to the text. *Shir* (as it is often called in abbreviated form) ceased being a human love story. Instead, it became a metaphor. Today, most commentators, particularly in liberal circles, return it to its original context and read it as a love story. Yet, while this original or more literal meaning is indispensable to this commentary, our aim is to provide modern liberal readers with a more spiritual reading of the text, raising it once again beyond the carnal to the more sacred level while recognizing the tension between the secular and the spiritual.

As we recognize this tension in the literature about the Song of Songs and the way various scholars navigate their way through the text, it is our goal, as liberal Jews, to hold both approaches in our minds and souls simultaneously. It is neither enough to recognize the text as erotic love poetry, nor to assign it to the relationship between God and Israel and forget its original intent altogether. Rather, we strive to see the beauty of the love poetry and its use as a spiritual metaphor for the relationship between God and the Jewish people, cast in the light of liberal Judaism. Admittedly, this is not an easy task, but we know that the result will help raise the spirits of all who are willing.

As a literary device, metaphor allows a text to be retained when a literal reading of the text—for one reason or another—has to be discarded. In the case of *Shir HaShirim*, the love story of a young woman and man was pushed aside and the text became a different love story: God's love for Israel. (Similarly, for Christians, it reflects Christ's love for his church.) It is this covenantal relationship that our commentary recaptures as it becomes a guide for the spiritual development of the reader.

While adding our own insights and comments in this volume, we also view the text through the lens of four different commentators: the *Targum* (ca. fifth-century Aramaic translation and interpretation of the Hebrew text); Rashi (1040–1105); Abraham ibn Ezra (1089–1164); and Gersonides (1288–1344). Since the *Targum* and Rashi reflect the notions of Rabbinic Judaism, their interpretations have much in common. The *Targum* is more than a translation of the Hebrew into Aramaic. It is also an interpretation of the text, which may include restatements as well as new elements clearly not intended by the original. This is particularly true in the *Targum* of the Song of Songs, where the erotic love poetry is constantly translated and interpreted within the context of the developing rabbinic interpretation of the text. Ibn Ezra and Gersonides, on the other hand, evidence the impact of philosophy on Judaism. Of all the commentators, Ibn Ezra consistently analyzes the text in the most literal fashion. Gersonides' interpretation of the text is even more directed, as he tries to use the text as an introduction to philosophy. Thus, his comments are used sparingly in this volume. While each commentator uses a different approach, they all deal with *Shir HaShirim* as a metaphor, even though they may be different metaphors. On occasion, we take guidance from the *Biblia Hebraica*, a familiar critical edition of the Bible edited by Rudolph Kittel and first published in 1905. We have also taken some direction from the critical scholarly work of L. H. Koehler and Walter Baumgartner's *Hebrew and Aramaic Lexicon of the Old Testament* (first published in 1948–1952).

Shir HaShirim is also referred to in English as Canticles and as the Song of Solomon. Eight chapters long, it is located in the third section of the Bible, known as Writings (*K'tuvim*). It is the first of five scrolls (*m'gillot*) contained in the Bible.

Because those who canonized the Bible had the clever ability to see the extended love poem as a model for the relationship between God and the individual, it is not surprising that the Song of Songs was eventually included in the *Kabbalat Shabbat* liturgy following the recital of *L'chah Dodi*. It was also read on Friday evening, because sex between married partners on Shabbat was encouraged by the Rabbis. Although the original text of the Song of Songs remained the same, as did its literal meaning, its extended meaning evolved over time, reflecting the experiences of the Jewish community. Nevertheless, its inclusion in the Bible was opposed by some because of its perceived secular character, which shares much with ancient Near Eastern love poetry, especially that from Egypt. Rabbi Akiva brought the discussion to a close by saying, "All the Writings are holy, but the Song of Songs is the holiest of all" (*Mishnah Yadayim* 3:5), intentionally using the term that refers to the inner sanctum, the holiest precinct, of the ancient Temple in Jerusalem. He understood its spiritual significance and its inherent power to fuel the relationship between the individual and God.

The relationship is classically described in terms of Israel as the bride and God as the bridegroom. This relationship became the foundation for the school of Jewish mysticism called *Merkavah* (chariot) mysticism, taking its name from the so-called chariot vision of the prophet Ezekiel (1:1–28). Some scholars argue that this symbolic mystical interpretation paved the way for individuals to develop a personal relationship with God through similar mystical approaches. This individual mysticism sees the bride of the Song of Songs as the human soul and her beloved as God. It is the insights drawn from this level of personal mysticism that we are trying to approximate in this commentary. Contemporary covenant theologians such as Rabbi Eugene Borowitz seek to emulate the model provided by the Song of Songs while not expressing it as graphically. Covenant theology assumes that the relationship (read: covenant) that was established between God and the congregation of Israel is mirrored in the relationship that individuals have with God. This relationship is best articulated as the I-Thou relationship, advanced by Martin Buber. Franz Rosenzweig used the Song of Songs in this way in his *The Star of Redemption* (bk. 2, ch. 2, pp. 199ff.).

Jewish tradition ascribes the Song of Songs to Solomon, written in the prime of his life. Scholars interpret Song of Songs 1:1 in various ways that direct its authorship to others, including King Hezekiah. Many assign it to the postexilic period because it includes one Persian loanword and many Aramaic ones. Similarly, scholars disagree as to whether it is a collection of individual love poems or a unified whole. Whatever its origins might have been, we have inherited it as one book and strive, as in our previous commentaries on sacred texts (such as *Pirkei Avot* and *Mishlei*), to understand it as one book.

Perhaps because spring reminds us of love and renewal, the Song of Songs is read in the synagogue during Pesach. Or perhaps it is because Passover celebrates the formative relationship between God and the Jewish people as they left Egypt and journeyed through the desert. As a reflection of this idea, Sephardim read the Song of Songs at the end of the Passover seder. But because the book reminds us of the power of love between humans and between humans and God, perhaps it should be read every day, a little at a time, so that as we grow in our understanding of the text, our relationship with God grows as well.

Shir HaShirim Rabbah

The midrash on the Song of Songs (called *Shir HaShirim Rabbah*), like the *Targum*, uses the Song of Songs as a lens through which it views Israel's historical record during the time of the Bible. It was composed in the Land of Israel, most probably in the sixth century C.E. The text includes a midrashic biography of Solomon and various additional interpretations of the Song of Songs. These interpretations—technically called hermeneutic principles—are grouped together at the end of the midrash on 1:1 and at the beginning of 1:2.

Shir HaShirim Zuta

Shir HaShirim Zuta, a small midrash on the Song of Songs, was first edited and published in 1894 by Solomon Schechter, who believed that it emerged originally in the ninth century. Other scholars place it earlier. The book, much more mystical than *Shir HaShirim Rabbah*, contains allusions to celestial visions and a messianic apocalypse, thus elevating the text from the physical to the metaphysical.

CHAPTER ONE

א:א שִׁיר הַשִּׁירִים אֲשֶׁר לִשְׁלֹמֹה:

1:1 THE SONG OF SONGS BY SOLOMON.

The *Targum* presents an early example of reading *Shir HaShirim* as more than simply a collection of love poems. It explains the opening verse as "the poems and praises that Solomon the prophet, king in Israel, moved by the spirit of prophecy, recited before the Master of the universe." According to Jewish tradition, these "poems and praises" form one of the ten songs of praise sung to the Creator by various biblical characters. The first song was sung by Adam on the occasion of the first Sabbath (Psalm 92). Moses sang the second song when the Re(e)d Sea was split (Exodus 15). The third song was sung by the Israelites when they received the moving well (Numbers 21). Moses sang the fourth song toward the end of his life (Deuteronomy 32). The fifth song was sung by Joshua on the occasion of the miracle at Gibeon (Joshua 10). Deborah and Barak sang the sixth song (Judges 5). Hannah sang the seventh (I Samuel 2). And David sang the eighth (generally identified as Psalm 18). Solomon sang the Song of Songs, the ninth song. And the tenth song will be sung by the exiles when they return to the Land during the time of the Messiah.

Rashi, in his comment, quotes Rabbi Akiva's puzzling comparison that the entire world was not as worthy as the day that *Shir HaShirim* was given to Israel. "All the Writings are holy," Akiva claimed, "but the Song of Songs is the holiest of all" (*Mishnah Yadayim* 3:5). Both Rashi and Akiva understand that the love between two people reflects the loving relationship—what theologians call the covenantal relationship—that an individual establishes with God. Ibn Ezra argues that although some scholars have attempted to see the Song of Songs as a metaphor of some kind of cosmic secret or as a metaphor expressing the link of the soul to the body, he will either read it literally or simply follow the accepted rabbinic interpretation. Gersonides, on the other hand, utilizes a play on the Hebrew words based on the root *sh-l-m*. He suggests that since *Shir HaShirim* was written by Solomon (*Sh'lomoh*), it is a clear indication that it deals with human perfection (*sh'leimut*). Not satisfied until he makes a philosophical point, Gersonides claims that the book is called the Song of Songs, that is, the best of songs, because it embodies two excellent qualities: it gives insight into esoteric matters, and it motivates the reader to love what is proper and, as a result, avoid what is not.

א:ב יִשָּׁקֵנִי מִנְּשִׁיקוֹת פִּיהוּ כִּי־טוֹבִים דֹּדֶיךָ מִיָּיִן:

1:2 KISS ME WITH THE KISSES OF YOUR MOUTH, FOR YOUR CARESSES ARE BETTER THAN WINE.

This gentle beginning provides a sense of the eroticism to follow. It also presents an immediate problem of style. The first clause is written in the third person (literally, "Let him kiss me with the kisses of his mouth"), and the second clause is written in the second person. Since 1:3 is written in the second person, we have chosen to translate the first clause of 1:2 that way as well. We believe that this is the overwhelming viewpoint taken in the entire text. But the verse also presents a question of gender. The author of the poem writes in the voice of a woman. It would therefore be inappropriate to translate the text in a gender-neutral manner. As a result, while we attempt to universalize the message throughout and express a sensitivity to gender in our translations of the Hebrew text, we have not tried to make our translations gender-free.

Dodecha (your caresses), which are described as "better than wine," suggests the familiar intoxication resulting from making love. This notion is repeated in 5:1, where the author advises us to *shichru dodim* (get drunk on caresses), and in Proverbs (7:18), also attributed to Solomon, where we read *l'chah nirveh dodim* ("let's get drunk on caresses" or "let's gorge ourselves on sex"). Those who have experienced spiritual "highs" readily understand this notion, even when the highs are physical.

The *Targum* explains this verse as a statement by Solomon in his role as a prophet, praising God for giving the Torah, the six orders of the Mishnah, and the Talmud to Moses in the same direct, face-to-face manner as one would kiss another. Thus, the *Targum* argues that "his mouth" is a reference to God and indirectly suggests the Oral Law.

Although Rashi takes this poem as a metaphor, as taught in the Talmud (*Shabbat* 63a, *Y'vamot* 24a), no verse ever loses its literal meaning completely. Thus, he interprets this verse as if the congregation of Israel, here personified as a young woman, says in her state of widowhood in exile that she yearns for the kisses she received as a bride—passionate kisses on the mouth rather than on the hand [or on the cheek or in the air].

Treating the verse more literally, Ibn Ezra takes *yishakeini* (let him kiss me) as the musings of the young woman who longs for many kisses. This notion, acknowledging that women enjoy sex as much as men do, is more acceptable today than it once was. However, Ibn Ezra also treats the verse as a metaphor and understands the words *yishakeini* and *n'shikot* (kisses) as referring to the Torah and mitzvot. He further suggests that the kisses began with Abraham, establishing and authenticating an early tradition that has been perpetuated throughout Jewish history.

For Gersonides, the poem is a parable of philosophy. He thus explains the verse as explaining the belief that the human intellect can unite with the Active Intellect. We might read this as an opening to making possible the mystery of union of the individual with God—what Chasidic tradition refer to as *d'veikus* (or *d'veikut,* literally, "sticking"), clinging to God.

א:ג לְרֵיחַ שְׁמָנֶיךָ טוֹבִים שֶׁמֶן תּוּרַק שְׁמֶךָ עַל־כֵּן עֲלָמוֹת אֲהֵבוּךָ:

1:3 YOUR PERFUME IS DELIGHTFUL TO SMELL. YOUR NAME
IS LIKE FRAGRANT OIL. THAT IS WHY YOUNG GIRLS
LOVE YOU.

The simple text suggests the musing of a young woman as she thinks of her lover. Read another way, this verse could also represent the reflections of the individual toward the sacred. Our translation of *shemen turak sh'mecha* as ''your name is like fragrant oil'' follows Ibn Ezra's view that the purpose of *shemen turak* (literally, ''oil poured forth'') is to release its fragrance. The *Targum*, however, understands the first clause as a reference to the many ''signs and wonders'' of the Divine that the Jewish people have experienced. These experiences continue to draw us to the Divine and motivate our spiritual search. Rashi understands the first clause as a reference to a good name (in other words, a good reputation) and the last clause as a reference to Jews-by-choice (like Jethro, Moses's father-in-law, whom the Rabbis saw as a righteous convert to Judaism). The verse is a philosophical metaphor, according to Gersonides, with the sense of smell as an allusion to the human desire to know God, and the perfume (literally, ''oils'') as a reference to the requisite sciences to be mastered so that the truth about the world can be known.

א:ד מָשְׁכֵנִי אַחֲרֶיךָ נָּרוּצָה הֱבִיאַנִי הַמֶּלֶךְ חֲדָרָיו נָגִילָה וְנִשְׂמְחָה בָּךְ
נַזְכִּירָה דֹדֶיךָ מִיַּיִן מֵישָׁרִים אֲהֵבוּךָ:

1:4 PULL ME AFTER YOU, LET'S RUN. THE KING HAS
BROUGHT ME INTO HIS ROOM. LET'S REJOICE AND BE
GLAD WITH YOU. LET'S REMIND OURSELVES THAT YOUR
CARESSES ARE BETTER THAN WINE. RIGHTLY, THEY
HAVE LOVED YOU.

Even the simple meaning of this verse presents problems and challenges our understanding of the text. Why does the author shift from second person to third person? Why is the king introduced as a subject in this verse? Is this, perhaps, some sort of love triangle? Maybe the young woman is playing a lover's game with her man. They seem to be going to a place where they will make love, and she pretends that she has been brought into the king's bedchamber to become a member of his harem. Her lover observes her there while other members of the harem praise her skills in the bedroom, as well as her beauty and charm.

Kittel, in his *Biblia Hebraica* (p. 1201), suggests that the word *chadarav* (his chambers or rooms) should be emended to *chadrecha* (your chamber or room) and that *hamelech* (the king) should be understood as what linguists call the vocative form (O king!). Thus, the clause would be read as ''O king, you have brought me to your room,'' and the remainder of the verse would be either the response of the ''king'' or the response of other members of the king's harem. Based on the reading of *dodim* discussed in verse 2, some scholars, including Kittel, have proposed emending *nazkirah dodecha* (let's remind ourselves [that] your caresses) to *nishk'rah dodecha* (let's get drunk [with] your caresses).

Using the image of the king as a metaphor for God, the *Targum* takes the verse to refer to "God's Presence" as leading the Israelites through the desert with a pillar of cloud by day and a pillar of fire at night on their way to Sinai to receive the Torah. Rashi similarly suggests that this provocative verse is a reference to the Israelites harking back to their original relationship with God, when, like a new bride, they committed themselves to God. Gersonides sees the verse as an indication of the various impediments to thought that must be overcome by the soul before the intellect can act. One such obstacle is bodily desire, symbolized by wine. Wine can be an impediment in any kind of relationship, particularly one with God. It can enhance the relationship, as it potentially does through *Kiddush*, or destroy it, as when one falls into a drunken stupor.

א:ה שְׁחוֹרָה אֲנִי וְנָאוָה בְּנוֹת יְרוּשָׁלָם כְּאָהֳלֵי קֵדָר כִּירִיעוֹת שְׁלֹמֹה:

1:5 I AM DARK BUT BEAUTIFUL, O DAUGHTERS OF JERUSALEM, LIKE THE TENTS OF KEDAR, LIKE THE CURTAINS OF SOLOMON.

Modern sensitivities alert us to a possible element of race embedded in the text. The author attempts to balance the statement by adding "beautiful" to "dark." However, it is clear from the translation of the *Targum* that "dark" is to be understood as "ugly," since it takes the verse as a metaphor describing the punishment suffered by the Israelites after the sin of the Golden Calf when the faces of the Israelites turned black. But this verse does not have to be read as making a comment about beauty or women of color. Rashi reads "dark" as a metaphor for the "darkness of the captivity of the people of Israel." Ibn Ezra suggests that dark means beautiful, but that "dark" is said (euphemistically) in order to avoid the evil eye. While it might have been tempting as well as grammatically correct to translate the "but" as "and" so that the statement reads simply "I am dark and beautiful," the verse that follows limits our ability to read this verse as a positive recognition of a multiracial Jewish history.

א:ו אַל־תִּרְאוּנִי שֶׁאֲנִי שְׁחַרְחֹרֶת שֶׁשְּׁזָפַתְנִי הַשָּׁמֶשׁ בְּנֵי אִמִּי נִחֲרוּ־בִי
שָׂמֻנִי נֹטֵרָה אֶת־הַכְּרָמִים כַּרְמִי שֶׁלִּי לֹא נָטָרְתִּי:

1:6 DON'T LOOK DOWN AT ME BECAUSE I HAVE BECOME
DARK. IT IS THE SUN THAT HAS SCORCHED ME. MY
MOTHER'S SONS WERE ANGRY WITH ME. THEY MADE ME
GUARD THE VINEYARDS, BUT MY OWN VINEYARD
I COULD NOT GUARD.

The speaker seems to be embarrassed by the color of her skin. The *Targum* continues the metaphor of darkness by suggesting that it represents punishment for sin. In this case, the people of Israel regret that they followed the advice of false prophets to worship the sun and the moon, causing them to forsake the Torah. As a result, they have incurred a harsh punishment from God, which is symbolized by "becoming dark." Our translation of *al tir-uni* (don't look down at me) follows Rashi and Ibn Ezra, who take the verse as a metaphor for sin and punishment. Rashi understands "my mother's sons" as a reference to the Egyptians, in whose midst the Israelites dwelt. Similarly, the "vine" stands for the idolatry for which the Israelites had forsaken their own Jewish practices. As might be expected, Gersonides assumes a philosophical posture by suggesting that "become dark" refers to all physical entities. By becoming material, and thus no longer part of the ethereal, spiritual world alone, they become corrupt, that is, imperfect. However, they are so attractive that they interfere with the ability of humans to attain perfection. For Gersonides, "my mother's sons" refers to those capacities within the soul that lead the individual to pursue pleasures of the body. "My own vineyard" is a reference to the proper reflection that leads to that sort of human perfection.

It seems clear that "dark" or "black" is not "beautiful" to the writer of the Song of Songs. Thus, there is some measure of latent and unintentional racism that needs to be overcome in our reading of the text and in our taking from it direction for our lives.

א:ז הַגִּידָה לִּי שֶׁאָהֲבָה נַפְשִׁי אֵיכָה תִרְעֶה אֵיכָה תַּרְבִּיץ בַּצָּהֳרָיִם
שַׁלָּמָה אֶהְיֶה כְּעֹטְיָה עַל עֶדְרֵי חֲבֵרֶיךָ:

1:7 TELL ME, MY SOUL'S DEAR LOVE, WHERE ARE YOU
GRAZING YOUR SHEEP? WHERE ARE YOU RESTING THEM
AT NOON? WHY SHOULD I BE AS ONE WHO IS LOST
NEAR THE FLOCKS OF YOUR FRIENDS?

The young woman who is speaking in the text turns to her beloved, who is presented in this poem as a shepherd. If she wants to meet her lover in the field, she has to know where he will be at lunchtime. The word *k'ot'yah* is somewhat problematic. If it is taken from the verb *atah* (hide or cover), the word then means "as someone veiled." However, what "someone veiled" would mean in this context is difficult to determine—unless the writer looks to Genesis 38:14–15, which suggests to us that the woman's desire for her lover is so overwhelming that she is willing to go after him. Others, like Koehler-Baumgartner (pp. 813–14), emend the word to *k'to-ah* from the verb *taah*, "to go astray, to be lost." We have followed this suggestion in our translation and understanding of the verse.

The *Targum* understands the behavior of the woman lover in the verse as a reference to Moses's final request to God. Prior to his death, Moses asks God to allow him to glimpse into Israel's future in order to ascertain how the people will endure their exile from the Land as well as their conflicts with the descendants of Ishmael. Rashi reads the verse as a conversation between spouses. One says to the other, "O God, how will You shepherd Your flock, the people of Israel, amidst the wolves of the nations? How will You protect them in exile?" Taking *k'ot'yah* to mean "as one veiled," Rashi continues. Speaking for the Israelites, Moses says, "It does not befit Your glory that I should go about veiled as a mourner bewailing their fate if You don't [care about them]." Ibn Ezra maintains that this verse reflects Israel's turning toward God in repentance. So we pursue God as humans, even as repentance is required of us in order to develop our relationship with the Divine. The human mirrors the Divine, even as we seek out a relationship with the Divine that mirrors the one we try to create with a spouse.

אִ:ח אִם־לֹא תֵדְעִי לָךְ הַיָּפָה בַּנָּשִׁים צְאִי־לָךְ בְּעִקְבֵי הַצֹּאן וּרְעִי אֶת־גְּדִיֹּתַיִךְ עַל מִשְׁכְּנוֹת הָרֹעִים:

1:8 O MOST BEAUTIFUL OF WOMEN, IF YOU DON'T KNOW, FOLLOW THE TRACKS OF THE FLOCK AND GRAZE YOUR KIDS NEAR THE TENTS OF THE SHEPHERDS.

The way this verse was written suggests that the writer might have wanted a chorus to speak these lines. What is unclear is why a woman yearning for her lover would want to meet him among other shepherds rather than alone. Since the *Targum* understood the previous verse as Moses's final plea to God at the end of his life, after being told he could not guide the Israelites into the Land of Israel, it reads this verse as God's answer. Moses will be able to see his "kids" from afar but will not be able to shepherd them into the Land. Rashi interprets this verse from the perspective of a shepherd who once had the responsibility to watch over this woman's sheep but no longer does. Nevertheless, he continues to advise her, caring for her and for her sheep. The shepherd tells her that if she wants to find grazing land, she will have to follow the tracks made by other sheep and their shepherds, and she will find appropriate grazing land where they made camp. Rashi then goes further and reads the verse as a response from the Divine Shepherd speaking to the flock, that is, the Jewish people as they wander among the nations. If they are to be preserved from all harm, then they must follow the example of their ancestors who accepted the Torah and observed the commandments. As their reward, their children will be able to live safely among the princes of the nations. Ibn Ezra's understanding of the verse is similar to Rashi's. He takes "flocks of your friends" (verse 7), however, as a reference to the temptations of apostasy. If the text is about nurturing a relationship with the Divine and the potential "pulls" that one has in life to go elsewhere and do other things, then the concern of the text and its author is especially well warranted.

א:ט לְסֻסָתִי בְּרִכְבֵי פַרְעֹה דִּמִּיתִיךְ רַעְיָתִי:

1:9 O MY DARLING, YOU ARE LIKE A MARE IN PHARAOH'S CHARIOTS.

While the modern reader may not regard these words as a compliment, the author of the text presumably meant them as such. In an extensive comment, however, the *Targum* interprets this verse as a reflection of the plight of the Israelites at the Red Sea. According to the metaphor constructed by the commentary, the sea is before them. The wilderness—filled with poisonous snakes—is to the right and left of them. Behind them, Pharaoh's army is in pursuit. God appears and dries up the waters of the sea but not the clay at its bottom. Some wicked people enrage God by suggesting that God could not dry up the clay. Moses, joined by the righteous people, prays and recites the Song of the Sea (Exodus 15:1–18) and assuages the wrath of God. Through the merit of their ancestors (*z'chut avot*), the Israelites are then able to cross on dry land.

Rashi, basing his comment on a particular verse from the prophet Habakkuk (3:15), believes that "the mare in Pharaoh's chariots" refers to the horses that God provided to counter those chariots and help deliver the Israelites. Ibn Ezra considers the "mare" differently, contending that it refers to the spoil that the escaping slaves took from their masters. In what is today an outdated comment, Gersonides believes that the author of the Song of Songs used the term "mare" (female horse) to indicate that male horses rule, just as male humans do, according to Genesis 3:16. To make his point, Gersonides suggests that the sexual act is a reflection of this notion: the male emits and the female receives. While we are sensitive to male-specific descriptions of God, especially when they place women in a subordinate position, it is difficult not to relate to the Divine in gender-specific terms. We strive to transcend such specificity, but the graphic illustration does make the relationship easier to imagine and understand. Men and women generally consider this relationship differently. While we have come to expect a more elevated philosophical comment from Gersonides, in this case he is simply reflecting the gender bias of his time.

א:י נָאווּ לְחָיַיִךְ בַּתֹּרִים צַוָּארֵךְ בַּחֲרוּזִים:

1:10 ORNAMENTED ROWS MAKE YOUR CHEEKS LOOK PRETTY, AS DOES A NECKLACE [ON] YOUR THROAT.

This could be a simple statement about the effect of jewelry on enhancing physical beauty. The *Targum* takes the "row" and the "necklace" as references to the bridle and bit used to direct an animal on its course. As metaphors, they refer to the words of Torah that direct the Jewish people. In this case, they might influence Moses to describe the people as "pretty." To carry the metaphor further, just as jewelry has the potential to enhance one's beauty, so does adorning oneself in the words of Torah enhance one's spiritual beauty. Ibn Ezra notes that the word *charuzim* means "necklace" occurs only in the Bible. In later Hebrew, the word refers to poetic rhymes. Continuing in his rather single-minded manner, Gersonides takes the verse as a reference to the intellect's ability to ascertain truth.

א:יא תּוֹרֵי זָהָב נַעֲשֶׂה־לָּךְ עִם נְקֻדּוֹת הַכָּסֶף:

1:11 WE WILL MAKE FOR YOU ORNAMENTED ROWS OF GOLD WITH INLAID POINTS OF SILVER.

The *Targum* relates this verse to the Revelation at Sinai. Moses ascended to heaven and received there two stone tablets hewn from the sapphire of the throne of glory, which had borders of fine gold. The Ten Commandments (literally "ten words" or "ten utterances") were written upon them. To the writer of the *Targum*, these "inlaid points" suggest the forty-nine ways, or hermeneutic principles, in which the Torah can be interpreted. The Rabbis used these principles to develop teaching sermons.

In Rashi's interpretation of the verse, we find an allusion to God enticing Pharaoh to pursue the Israelites into the wilderness while carrying with him all the riches of the royal treasury. As a result, the escaping slaves were able to take these riches with them. Thus, the "inlaid points" indicate the amount of the spoil. Following the *Targum*'s interpretation of the previous verse, Ibn Ezra refers the verse to the elaborate bridles and bits on Pharaoh's horses. These images of beauty from a previous era can be hard to imagine. Having been created in the image of God, we are dealing with more than simple surface beauty when we try to enhance our beauty or that of others. We are working to enhance the relationship between ourselves and God through our relationships with others.

א:יב עַד־שֶׁהַמֶּלֶךְ בִּמְסִבּוֹ נִרְדִּי נָתַן רֵיחוֹ:

1:12 WHILE THE RULER IS AT THE BANQUET TABLE, MY NARD PROVIDES A FRAGRANCE.

While the verse appears to be simple and straightforward, it is actually rather difficult. We have moved completely away from the sense of the previous verse. There seems to be a new narrator, though it is unclear who it is. Similarly, we cannot identify this ruler. Perhaps the young woman who has been previously narrating the text is speaking to her lover. Perhaps she is speaking to Solomon, the supposed author of the book. Since we are not sure where the conversation is taking place or who is speaking, the meaning of *bim'sibo* (his banquet table or cushion) is uncertain. Maybe, instead of this incident taking place in a real palace, it occurs in an imagined palace or in a lover's hideaway. We assume that "nard" is related to *nirdi,* an aromatic drug used for its perfume, that is made from a plant that grows in the Himalayas, but we don't know whether *reicho* (its or his fragrance) refers to the perfume or to the ruler/lover. In our translation, we have decided that the fragrance refers to the young woman's lover and thus we have taken the phrase *natan reicho* (provides a fragrance) as the proud statement of the young woman who provides pleasure to her lover through her own fragrance. The *Targum* picks up on the word *ad* (while) and suggests that the verse refers to the events at Sinai: while Moses was on top of the mountain receiving the Ten Commandments, certain wicked people among the Israelites built the Golden Calf. Such an idolatrous act was thought to be so vile that it actually smelled. Thus, the fragrance of virtue became the stench of vice. Rashi also sees this verse as a reference to the incident of the Golden Calf and reads it as the confession of the Israelites that evil had taken the place of good. Both Rashi and the *Targum* take *nirdi* to be an unpleasant odor. Ibn Ezra, however, sees the verse as foreshadowing the advent of the Messiah. At that time, the Israelites will be brought to the mountain of God and will delight in the smell of the incense offered in the rebuilt Temple.

א:יג צְרוֹר הַמֹּר דּוֹדִי לִי בֵּין שָׁדַי יָלִין:

1:13 MY BELOVED IS MY BAG OF MYRRH RESTING BETWEEN MY BREASTS.

It seems clear that the author intends the phrase *bein shadai yalin* (resting between my breasts) to refer both to a "bag of myrrh" and to "my beloved." The author notes again that the sense of smell is important in making love. The *Targum* meanwhile continues with its connection to the Golden Calf story: Moses is to descend from Mount Sinai after being told that his people have become corrupt. He asks God's mercy for the people and invokes the near sacrifice of Isaac (the *Akeidah* or *Akeidat Yitzchak*) as a reason for mercy. While Rashi also sees the verse as a reference to the sin of the Golden Calf, he understands it to refer specifically to God's forbearance and forgiveness. When the people offer gold for the building of the Sanctuary, he argues, they will atone for the Golden Calf. Ibn Ezra takes "between my breasts" to refer to the two cherubim that were to stand above the ark cover of the Sanctuary (Exodus 25:8–22). None of the commentators deal significantly with the erotic nature of the verse, with its image of snuggling between the fragrant breasts of a lover. Perhaps had they considered the potential for a truly intimate relationship with the Divine, the images would have been allowed to speak to them directly, so that the image of breasts used in this verse could be understood as a reference to the nurturing presence of God.

אֶשְׁכֹּל הַכֹּפֶר דּוֹדִי לִי בְּכַרְמֵי עֵין גֶּדִי: א:יד

1:14 MY BELOVED IS MY CLUSTER OF HENNA BLOOMS FROM THE VINEYARDS OF EIN GEDI.

Since henna has become a part of popular culture in North America, its use in enhancing beauty is more recognizable than it might have been some years ago, when its use was primarily limited to the Near East. Playing on the word *hakofer* (henna blooms), the *Targum* establishes a relationship to its homonym meaning "the ransom" or "the atonement" and continues to retell the story of the Golden Calf. Moses descends from the mountain, drops the tablets, burns the calf, mixes its ashes with water, forces the Israelites to drink the mixture, executes the guilty, ascends again to heaven, and receives another set of tablets. Then Moses prays to God and gains atonement for *(v'kaper)* or ransoms the Israelites by having them build a Sanctuary. There the forgiven people will offer a sacrifice together with the offering of wine produced at Ein Gedi. In an uncharacteristically short comment Rashi simply notes that *kofer* is some sort of spice, while Ibn Ezra suggests that it is some kind of dried date.

הִנָּךְ יָפָה רַעְיָתִי הִנָּךְ יָפָה עֵינַיִךְ יוֹנִים: א:טו

1:15 OH, YOU ARE BEAUTIFUL, MY DARLING, YOU ARE BEAUTIFUL. YOUR EYES ARE LIKE THOSE OF DOVES!

The comparison presents difficulties. Perhaps the writer is trying to compare the color or the luminescence of his lover's eyes with those of a dove. Regarding the word "beautiful," the *Targum* notes that when the Israelites followed the will of God, they merited the praise of all the angels. Thus, the first "beautiful" refers to their adherence to the commandments. The second "beautiful" refers to their study of Torah. Furthermore, "doves" suggests that the Israelites have become as holy as sacrificial doves offered on the altar. For Rashi, this verse is a metaphor for God's consoling words to the Israelites that their sins have been forgiven (Numbers 14:20). The phrase "your eyes are like those of doves" suggests to Rashi that just as clear eyes indicate physical health, so Israel has religious leaders—the eyes of the community—who will lead them to spiritual health. "Doves" presents an additional notion: just as doves are ever true to their mates, so those leaders are forever true to God

הִנְּךָ יָפֶה דוֹדִי אַף נָעִים אַף־עַרְשֵׂנוּ רַעֲנָנָה: א:טז

1:16 O MY BELOVED, YOU ARE HANDSOME AND BEAUTIFUL, AND OUR BED IS SHADED BY LEAVES.

This verse suggests that the lovers are beneath a tree, out in the field. In its commentary on the verse, the *Targum* takes a liberty by adding this response by the Israelites to God: "When Your Presence is with us, when You accept our prayers with favor, when You increase our children, then we shall grow and increase like a tree planted by a spring of water whose branches are mighty and whose leaves are many." Rashi also takes the verse as a response by the Israelites. As an interpretation of the verse, he has them saying, "You are the One who is beautiful because You forgave us and again placed Your Presence among us." Rashi takes "our bed" as a reference to the progeny of Israel, who gathered before God in the Sanctuary and in the Temple.

א:יז קֹרוֹת בָּתֵּינוּ אֲרָזִים רחיטנו רַהִיטֵנוּ בְּרוֹתִים:

1:17 THE BEAMS OF OUR HOUSE ARE CEDARS, OUR RAFTERS
ARE JUNIPER.

Usually translated as "cypress," our translation of *b'rotim* as "juniper" follows Koehler-Baumgartner (p. 155). Following the previous verse, with its image of "a bed shaded by leaves," the writer describes the lovers as surrounded by a variety of trees in this verse. Perhaps such a wooded area existed in ancient Jerusalem, or maybe the lovers are simply in the best imaginable, if unreal, place. The *Targum* puts the verse in the mouth of Solomon, who praises the Temple in Jerusalem, as well as the Temple that will, according to Jewish tradition, be built when the Messiah arrives. While Rashi admits that he does not know the precise meaning of *rahiteinu* (our rafters), he suggests that the verse is related to the Sanctuary. Thus, the word refers to either bars or boards. Ibn Ezra supports Rashi by noting that the word appears nowhere else in the Bible.

The Moving Well

The Rabbis (Babylonian Talmud, *Taanit* 9a; *Shir HaShirim Rabbah* 4:14, 27; see also Rashi on Numbers 20:2) suggest that the water that sustained the people of Israel during their journey through Sinai—and disappeared when Miriam died—came from a miraculous well created during the twilight on the eve of the first Sabbath that traveled with the people for forty years in the desert. According to the midrash, it was given to Miriam by God because of her holiness. The water from Miriam's Well, as it was called, cured body and soul in addition to quenching the thirst of the Israelites. Miriam and her well provided ongoing spiritual oases in the desert.

The Miracle at Gibeon

During the period of Joshua's leadership, the sun is said to have stood still in the sky over Gibeon (on the third of Tammuz) as Joshua's army fought a mighty battle against the enemies of the Israelites. The event is described in the Book of Joshua (10:12–14).

Active Intellect/Hylic Intellect

While the exact meaning of the term "intellect" differs depending on context and the specific vocabulary of writers (philosophers/theologians), Aristotle spoke of separate intellects, the spiritual and nonmaterial entities derived from the highest spiritual being. The active intellect was divine, while the hylic intellect was seated in the material world of the human. Philosophers such as Alexander of Aphrodias defined Aristotle's active intellect as that aspect of the Divine with which the human being could connect. Because of the specific technical meaning of the term, it took on a religious dimension: knowledge of God leads to union with God. Human perfection, perhaps even immortality, is a direct result of such communion with the Divine. The idea that the human soul could realize its highest potential as the acquired intellect became dominant is found in the philosophy of Moses Maimonides and his followers. Proponents of this view—and of the rationalist approach underlying it—sought an intellectual understanding of God rather than an emotional one expressed in terms of love.

Six Orders of the Mishnah and Talmud

The so-called Oral Law was systematically codified first into the Mishnah by Rabbi Y'hudah HaNasi (ca. 200 C.E.) and then into the Talmud (ca. 400 C.E.). There were other collections, which came to be known as *baraitot*, or "other mishnahs," but his became authoritative. While various laws are scattered throughout the Torah, Rabbi Y'hudah HaNasi arranged these laws according to various topics. He assembled sixty-three tractates (*masechtot*, literally, "woven fabric") into six major sections (called "orders"). These orders are *Z'ra-im* (seeds, focusing primarily on agricultural laws but including tractates such as *B'rachot*, blessings); *Mo-eid* (appointed times, like holidays and seasons); *Nashim* (women, presenting issues between men and women, as well as laws of marriage and divorce); *N'zikin* (damages, a summary of civil and criminal law); *Kodashim* (holy things, an outline of the laws of sacrifices and ritual slaughter); and *Tohorot* (pure things, a concentration on the laws of ritual purity and impurity). The tractates are subdivided into chapters and then further divided into individual mishnah paragraphs, also called *halachot*. While much of the Mishnah reads as dry legal material and is not organized as straightforwardly as Rabbi Y'hudah HaNasi thought it to be, he made the text more interesting by including minority opinions in order to promote future scholarly discussion.

Oral Law and Written Law

According to rabbinic tradition, Moses received the Written Law *(Torah Shebichtav)* on Mount Sinai along with an Oral Law *(Torah Sheb-al Peh)*. While the Written Law was quickly written down, the Oral Law was transmitted orally for centuries until it eventually took the form of the Talmud (a combination of Mishnah and Gemara) around 400 C.E. The word *mishnah* (from the Hebrew *shanah*, "to repeat") hints at the method of repetition and memorization that was used to transmit the legal material from one generation to another. The notion of an Oral Law helped the Rabbis wrestle community authority away from the priests, whose authority rested in the Written Law. Following the destruction of the Temple in 70 C.E., this challenge to authority became moot. Whether or not the Rabbis used the Oral Law as a political device, it is clear that the laws of the Torah could not be obeyed without the details of their observance that are articulated in the Talmud.

Jethro

When Moses escapes into Midian, following the incident in which he slays an Egyptian taskmaster, he marries Zipporah, one of the local priest's daughters (Exodus 2). As a result, Moses becomes a shepherd for Jethro, Zipporah's father. The relationship between son-in-law and father-in-law grows, and Jethro becomes a spiritual counselor and legal adviser to Moses (Exodus 18). The Rabbis are uncomfortable with this role for a non-Israelite and therefore transform Jethro in the midrash into a proselyte par excellence.

Pillar of Cloud and Pillar of Fire

According to the biblical text, God used a pillar of cloud and a pillar of fire to guide the Israelites throughout their journey through the Sinai desert following their exodus from Egyptian slavery. The cloud was their guide by day; the fire served them at night (Exodus 13:21–22). While one tradition suggests that an angel led the cloud, a second tradition holds that God's Presence was contained in the cloud, seeing it as a constant vehicle for divine revelation throughout the desert journey. Following the construction of the desert Tabernacle, the cloud (as the Divine Presence) covers the Tabernacle and there takes up a permanent dwelling of sorts. Afterward, the ascent or descent of the cloud indicated to the Israelites when to stop and when to move forward on their journey.

The Evil Eye

As a part of popular folklore, the notion of the Evil Eye (in Hebrew, *Ayin Hara*) suggested that an individual has the power to harm people by looking at them. Young children and pregnant women were thought to be particularly vulnerable. Protective measures against the curse of the Evil Eye included the use of salt, specific amulets, the colors red or blue, specific hand gestures, the number five, and saying the opposite of a person's positive attribute. While certain people (like the biblical Joseph, who was considered to be naturally blessed) and certain animals (like fish, similarly blessed) were safe from the Evil Eye, people struck by it could perform specific rituals to remove its influence over them.

Merit of the Ancestors

The traditional notion of the merit of the ancestors *(z'chut avot)* suggests that the pious deeds of parents ensure blessings for their descendants. It is expressed in the text of the Ten Commandments (Exodus 20:6) as God showing "kindness to the thousandth generation of those who love Me and keep My commandments." The Rabbis of the midrash apply this principle extensively to the Patriarchs (and we would add the Matriarchs). This idea was extended in the Middle Ages to include the pious deeds of children *(z'chut banim)* as benefiting deceased parents.

Throne of Glory

The image of the throne of glory emerges from several specific biblical texts, including I Kings 22:19, where the prophet Micaiah tells King Jehoshaphat, "I saw *Adonai* seated upon the throne, with all the host of heaven standing in attendance to the right and to the left." The notion of a throne of glory emphasizes the idea of divine majesty, of God as a sovereign ruler. Even the Ark of the Covenant includes imagery of a throne. In one of Ezekiel's most vivid images, he reported seeing a divine throne as a chariot accompanied by strange creatures. This passage from Ezekiel 1:1–28 became the foundation for a significant school of Jewish mysticism.

Hermeneutic Principles

Hermeneutic principles are rules for the interpretation of the biblical text for halachic (legal) and aggadic (nonlegal, parable) purposes. These principles eventually took shape as the thirteen *midot* (principles) of Rabbi Yishmael ben Elisha, although they were first classified by Hillel, who formulated only seven basic principles. Rabbi Eliezer ben Yosei HaG'lili expanded Rabbi Yishmael's set into thirty-two. These *midot* constitute the basis of the legal nexus between the Oral and Written Law. While we may speak of an "Oral" Law, because it was transmitted in oral form for many years, it is clear that the legal material in it was derived by the application of these principles to the Written Law.

Golden Calf

There are those who argue that it would be easier to appreciate God's Presence were they able to see the results of it firsthand. Yet, the generation of the Exodus—who witnessed their deliverance from Egypt—built the Golden Calf, an idol, less than two months after their miraculous release from Egyptian slavery. As narrated in Exodus 32, Moses ascended Mount Sinai to receive the Law from God and tarried there for forty days. The Israelites grew impatient and demanded that Aaron fashion a god for them. Perhaps thinking that the people would be reluctant to do so, Aaron asked them to gather their jewelry together—which, according to legend, they had taken as Egyptian spoil when they left the country—and Aaron molded it into the Golden Calf.

As a result, God's fury was ignited. This anger was probably fueled by the orgy-like behavior (as reported in Exodus 32:6, "and they rose to make merry") more than by their seeming idolatry. Like a parent, God redressed Moses about the Israelites' actions, asking him about *his* children, claiming no responsibility for the people. In turn, Moses confronted Aaron, who did not feel at all accountable for the act, as he threw the jewelry into the fire and it came out as a calf, formed from gold (Exodus 32:21–24). Showing great leadership, Moses cast his own lot with the people and bid God to punish him along with the people. As a result of Moses's stand, God made a commitment to punish only those who had sinned.

GLEANINGS

Meditation before the Song of Songs

So here I am, O' One I am to love with all my heart,
Waiting to be damaged by love's selflessness
or destructive through its selfishness.
Where once there was fragrance
And melody and form,
Softness and sweet,
Now only glamour remains.
Let me trust again in love's naïve ability
To restore my soul.
Let it be for me; for the one I love; for Your sake.
May the uniting of one lover with another
fashion a like union in the highest orders of Being,
Reuniting male and female dimensions
Of Your holiness.
The six days of creation
With the seventh day of *Shabbat,*
Sun with moon, daylight with night dark,
Insight with intuition,
Sending with receiving, having with being,
What can be told with what cannot, right with left.
Sides not only of Your holiness, but within myself.
Let me remember, One of Unity,
That all the ways of one in love
Are also the ways of Your Torah:
Affection and ecstasy,
Song and whisper,
Sharing, creating, being at once parent and child.
Surely, as it has been taught of old,

The day of the giving of the Song of Songs
Was the holiest day.
Holy One of Being, let me awaken
To the dew of my youth.
Let me be worthy to live again on the holiest day.
Let me belong to my beloved
And let my beloved belong to me.

Lawrence Kushner, *Eyes Remade for Wonder: A Lawrence Kushner Reader*
(Woodstock, VT: Jewish Lights, 1998), 203–4

So Many Kinds of Love

So many kinds of love. When we are courageous we enter each day, each relationship, seeing within it the possibilities for arousal, for devotion, for feelings powerful enough to overwhelm.

What a dangerous way to live, to live as a lover. So we learn to be wise, with our feelings, with our fingers, we learn to be careful. Women especially are taught to be careful, are urged to be careful.

What have I wanted to teach my daughter, my son, about love? And what have I already taught in a thousand ways when I was just living, living my ordinary day-to-day life, unaware how my every move was being recorded, catalogued, deconstructed. What did I learn growing up in my childhood home?

I knew my mother loved my father because she never challenged him, never confronted him. She treated him respectfully. It was her way.

I knew my father loved my mother because on an ordinary...morning, if a Cole Porter song came on the radio, he would put his newspaper down, take the dustcloth from her hand, and there in the living room with the morning sunlight streaming through the windows, he'd dance with her. It was his way.

And what is my way? I have many ways—of showing love, of feeling love, of expressing love. Many ways of taking it in, many ways of shutting it out, many openings to arousal.

Merle Feld, *A Spiritual Life: A Jewish Feminist Journey*
(Albany, NY: State University of New York Press, 1999), 87

Zekhut

Zekhut is usually translated "merit." In the heavenly balancing of good and evil deeds, it is the "credit" we receive on the side of the good. This *zekhut* may be because of an entire life of piety or because of some single half-forgotten good deed done long ago. It may be the result of *tsedakah* given in our own name or could derive from the great merit of an ancestor or relative. It may simply be part of the *zekhut* that belongs to all Jews because we are descendants of the *avot* [patriarchs], whose store of divine blessing is never exhausted.

Zekhut is also used in the sense of a special privilege we are rarely given. This might be the privilege of meeting or hearing a wise or great person, or the rare opportunity to perform the sort of *mitsvah* or an act of *tikkun 'olam* [world repair] that few of us have the chance to fulfill. In such moments, we might be tempted to say the words of the students of Rabbi Simeon ben Yohai, after he has taught them some profound secret of *Kabbalah* [Jewish mysticism]: "Blessed are we. Had we come into the world only for this moment, it would have been sufficient."

Arthur Green, *These Are the Words: A Vocabulary of Jewish Spiritual Life*
(Woodstock, VT: Jewish Lights, 1999), 145

A Religion of Love

Judaism has often been described as a religion of law; yet few of its commandments are as central to Judaism as is *ahavat ha-El*, the love of God. On this score the Torah is uncommonly emphatic, putting a threefold stress upon our duty, an excess typical of true love: "You"—singular—"shall love the Lord your God with all your heart, with all your soul, and with all your might" (Deut. 6:5). By what spiritual genius did this sentence follow immediately upon: "Hear, O Israel, *Adonai* is our God, *Adonai* is One" (Deut. 6:4)? (Of course, this was not yet "The *Shema*," as it came to be in postbiblical days.) But to say that *Adonai* is the Only One, the Unique, the Whole, the Primary, is to indulge in a passion of admiration and exclusivity that parallels what can happen between two people.

By the rabbinic era, the *Shema* was a critical component of the prayers we say twice each day. Each time we recite these prayers, we engage in a dialogue of love. For not only do we follow the *Shema* by recounting the command to love God, but we always introduce the *Shema* with prayers reminding us of God's love for us. Thus in the evening we say: *Barukh atah Adonai, ohev amo Yisrael*, Blessed are You, *Adonai*, who loves Your people Israel; and in the morning service we say: *Barukh atah Adonai, ha-boḥer be-amo Yisrael be-ahavah*, Blessed are You, *Adonai*, who in love chooses Your people Israel. The heart of Jewish prayer is this affirmation of our mutual love.

Eugene B. Borowitz and Frances Weinman Schwartz, *The Jewish Moral Virtues*
(Philadelphia: Jewish Publication Society, 1999), 316

CHAPTER TWO

:בּ:א אֲנִי חֲבַצֶּלֶת הַשָּׁרוֹן שׁוֹשַׁנַּת הָעֲמָקִים

2:1 I AM THE ROSE OF SHARON, THE LILY OF THE VALLEYS.

It is difficult to accurately identify the flowers mentioned in the text: *chavatzelet* (rose) and *shoshanah* (lily). Suffice it to say that the author is describing beautiful flowers. According to Koehler-Baumgartner, the first flower is "asphodel" (p. 287) and the second is "lily" (p. 1455). However, the *Targum* translates the first as *narkis* (white daffodil) and the second as *varda* (rose). According to the *Targum*, the verse means that whenever the Divine Presence rested upon Israel, the flowers could be compared to those that grew in the Garden of Eden. Rashi does not assist in horticultural identification; however, he takes *chavatzelet* to mean *shoshanah*, explaining that *shoshanat ha-amakim* is the same flower, which is more beautiful when it grows in the moist soil of the valleys than when it grows in the more arid soil of the hills. Ibn Ezra reflects the uncertain identification of *chavatzelet* in noting that some regard it as a rose and others say that it is a beautiful dark flower with a marvelous aroma. He offers two possibilities for *shoshanah* as well: according to some, it is a rose; according to others, it is a white flower whose aroma is so powerful that it causes headaches.

:בּ:ב כְּשׁוֹשַׁנָּה בֵּין הַחוֹחִים כֵּן רַעְיָתִי בֵּין הַבָּנוֹת

2:2 LIKE A LILY AMONG THORNS, SO IS MY DARLING AMONG
THE OTHER WOMEN.

The *Targum* continues its explanation from the previous verse: the Divine Presence rests upon the people of Israel when they follow God's ways. However, the Presence will be removed should they turn away. They will then become subject to the evil decrees of the nations (the "thorns"). Reading *shoshanah* here as "rose," Rashi interprets the verse to mean that although the "thorns" may prick the "rose," it remains beautiful in its redness. Likewise, "my darling"—the people of Israel—will remain true to the one God, although they are tempted to whore after other gods. Gersonides understands the verse to mean that when the other psychic capacities are subservient to the intellect, they will help it achieve perfection. However, they will keep it from achieving the perfection should they turn toward physical pleasures.

ב:ג כְּתַפּוּחַ בַּעֲצֵי הַיַּעַר כֵּן דּוֹדִי בֵּין הַבָּנִים בְּצִלּוֹ חִמַּדְתִּי וְיָשַׁבְתִּי
וּפִרְיוֹ מָתוֹק לְחִכִּי׃

2:3 Like an apple tree among other trees of the field, so is my beloved among the other boys. With great delight I sat in his shadow, and his fruit was sweet to my mouth.

While the analogy from the previous verse continues, the *Targum* changes the tree and the fruit. It reads: just as the *etrog* (that is, the *etrog* tree) is more desirable than those trees that bear no fruit, so the Holy One gained more praise among the angels when God revealed God's Self at Mount Sinai and gave the Torah to the people. Its words are sweet to their palate; they shall receive a reward in the world-to-come. Rashi and Ibn Ezra take *tapuach* to mean "apple," but Rashi follows the *Targum* in its reference to the theophany at Mount Sinai. For Gersonides, just as the apple tree may be negatively affected in its growth by other trees, here it stands for an individual's psychic capacities, which can be negatively affected by other people.

It is clear from this verse and others that the Bible is not afraid of explicit sexual imagery. In Judaism, sex within the context of a loving relationship is celebrated. Using sensual, graphically erotic images, the author is painting a word picture of pleasure, one that cannot easily be emulated in the relationship that the individual has with God. However, there are some who maintain that the traditional choreography of prayer mimics various aspects of the physical relationship between lovers.

ב:ד הֱבִיאַנִי אֶל־בֵּית הַיָּיִן וְדִגְלוֹ עָלַי אַהֲבָה׃

2:4 He brought me into the tavern and his banner of love is over me.

This seemingly simple verse proves to be difficult to translate and analyze. Here, the writer abruptly changes context: the young woman who is narrating her love story takes us from the outdoors of the previous verse to the inside of a tavern (literally, "house of wine"). Perhaps the speaker wants to make their relationship public, but a tavern does not seem like the best place to do so. If the lover is a king who brought his lover into his chambers (see 1:4), then any public place would expose their relationship. If the writer means to imply that the lover is indeed the king, then would a king bring his beloved to a local bar? If he were traveling in disguise, then he would not be revealing their relationship. This puzzling verse becomes even more complicated as we try to ascertain the meaning of *diglo* (his banner). It is possible that taverns of old resembled contemporary lounges that advertise their beverages on signs hanging outside. Or perhaps the "sign" is a metaphor for his love for her. However, there is no evidence of such usage elsewhere in the Bible. Kohler-Baumgartner (p. 213) takes *diglo* as a verb to mean "he contemplates; he examines me." While the commentators avoid discussing it, perhaps the verse is simply an erotic metaphor suggesting that he brought his love into the privacy of a tavern and enveloped her there with his body in an act of love. Thus, the verse would be about making the love private, not public.

The *Targum* takes the verse as the happy statement of the Israelites, personified as a young woman, who tells of being brought into the study house of Sinai to learn words of Torah from Moses. The "banner," then, would stand for all the commandments of the Torah, which were lovingly accepted by the Israelites. Rashi interprets the "house of wine" as the Tent of Meeting, in which Israel learned the details of the Torah. He understands "the banner" as a reference to Jewish communities in which love for God was manifested. Ibn Ezra also takes "his banner" to refer to Jewish communities. For Gersonides, the "house of wine" refers to the physical pleasures to which we are attracted. The "banner" is that which is raised by the hylic (material) intellect as it forsakes such pleasures and pursues philosophical perfection instead, while "love" refers to the intense pleasure that is experienced when attaining perfection.

ב:ה סַמְּכוּנִי בָּאֲשִׁישׁוֹת רַפְּדוּנִי בַּתַּפּוּחִים כִּי־חוֹלַת אַהֲבָה אָנִי:

2:5 SUSTAIN ME WITH RAISIN CAKES; REFRESH ME WITH APPLES; FOR I AM LOVESICK.

"Raisin cakes" have an idolatrous cultic use in Hosea 3:1, which the prophet decries. However, perhaps the writer wanted to suggest something more than a folk remedy for lovesickness. The writer presents a woman who declares her love in this verse—an act that is generally not recorded in biblical texts about women. We read of Isaac's love for Rebekah in the Torah, but we know nothing of her feelings for him. We know that Jacob loved Rachel more than he loved Leah, but we don't know anything about the sisters' love for Jacob. The only romantic love of a woman for a man that appears overtly in the Bible is that of Michal's for David.

In the *Targum*, this verse refers to the revelation at Sinai once again. Overwhelmed by the word spoken out of the fire, the people of Israel ask Moses and Aaron to receive that word and to bring them to the house of study so that they may be sustained by the words of Torah. These words perfume the world and are as delightful as are the taste of the apples that grew in the Garden of Eden. Rashi views the passage more literally, suggesting that the raisin cakes made of fine flour are the proper kind of food for those who are ill, since they emit the odor of apples, thought to possess a healing property. Ibn Ezra connects the raisin cakes and apples to the house of wine from the previous verse. If the house of wine is some kind of tavern, then the cakes and apples are the poets who are found in such taverns. Gersonides replays his philosophical analysis in which the intellect again speaks of its desire for union and perfection. The raisin cakes and apples, therefore, refer to the intellect's appeal to other aspects of the soul for assistance in its quest.

בּ:וּ שְׂמֹאלוֹ תַּחַת לְרֹאשִׁי וִימִינוֹ תְּחַבְּקֵנִי׃

2:6 Would that his left hand be beneath my head
and his right hand embrace me.

This verse intimates a physical description of lovemaking. Since the author included the verb with suffix *t'chab'keini* (embrace me) in the imperfect (future) tense, we understand it to suggest a future hope, the expression of a lovesick girl, although the grammar also allows us to take it as a present state. Rather than understanding the verse as describing the physical act of love, the *Targum* notes that the verse describes the protection afforded the Israelites upon entering the wilderness. They were protected from all kinds of harm, because they were surrounded by the clouds of glory (pillars of cloud and fire). Rashi takes the verse as the yearning of a lovesick Israel in exile, remembering that in the wilderness God had protected the people and provided them with manna and quail. For Ibn Ezra, the "left hand...beneath my head" literally suggests that the lover in the story is willing to present his love openly. Ibn Ezra states further that on a symbolic level, the verse refers to the morning and evening sacrificial offerings in the Temple. Gersonides also reads the verse on two levels. He suggests that it reminds us of the close physical contact effected when two people are making love. Symbolically, he thinks that the left hand is a reference to *yetzer hara* (the evil inclination), as well as to *Samael* (Satan)—physical desire. He argues that the author has already alluded to such physical desires in previous verses (by "thorns" [2:2] and "the trees of the field" [2:3]). For him, the right hand refers to *yetzer hatov* (the good inclination).

בּ:ז הִשְׁבַּעְתִּי אֶתְכֶם בְּנוֹת יְרוּשָׁלַ͏ִם בִּצְבָאוֹת אוֹ בְּאַיְלוֹת הַשָּׂדֶה
אִם־תָּעִירוּ וְאִם־תְּעוֹרְרוּ אֶת־הָאַהֲבָה עַד שֶׁתֶּחְפָּץ׃

2:7 O daughters of Jerusalem, I charge you, by the
roes or the hinds of the field: don't wake,
don't excite love until it pleases.

In order to understand this verse, we must first determine why the author (writing for the lover or the narrator of this love story) charges Jewish women by the "roes or the hinds of the field." Because of the verb *hishbia* (to cause to swear), it might be expected that the writer would invoke the Deity (such as in Genesis 24:3), rather than animals. Moreover, what do the animals mentioned here have to do with love? Perhaps the words *tz'vaot* (roes) and *ay'lot* (hinds) suggest more than animals. The *Targum* takes the words as divine names, as in the formula *Adonai Tz'vaot* (Lord of Hosts) and *T'kufei ar-a d'Yisrael* (the Almighty of the Land of Israel). Is the author of the text hinting that these words refer to other deities? We know that *tz'va hashamayim* refers to the heavenly host (Koehler-Baumgartner, p. 995). It could be that *tz'vaot* refers to these heavenly hosts as well. *Ayil* can mean "ruler," "mighty," and "ram" (Koehler-Baumgartner, p. 40). *Ay'lot hasadeh* could therefore be a reference to female deities of the field. That would help clarify that whoever "charge[s]" the "daughters of Jerusalem" does so by invoking the "hosts of heaven" and the "goddesses of the field."

As noted, the *Targum* takes *Tz'vaot* and *Ay'lot* as divine names, placing them in a speech delivered by Moses to the people after the advance team—the so-called spies—returned from Canaan with a bad report (Numbers 14:33). That report would delay the entrance into the Land for forty years (although the Rabbis of the midrash cite a variety of reasons for the delay, including the sin of the Golden Calf). As a result, Moses warned the people, invoking the names of the Lord of Hosts and the Almighty of the Land. He told them that until they received a favorable response from God, they should not even try to enter, lest they court the kind of disaster that befell the tribe of Ephraim. Ibn Ezra cites this same story, but Rashi contends that those being warned are the nations in whose midst Israel lives. The mention of "roes" and "hinds," he concludes, is a subtle suggestion that these animals are always in danger of being killed and eaten. Similarly, any nation that interferes with the relationship between God and the Jewish people puts itself at risk. Gersonides takes the word "charge" to indicate the intellect's great desire for perfection. He reads the words "roe" and "hind"—names for swift animals—as symbols for the intellect's desire to rush to that perfection without proceeding properly, step by step. Just as two lovers may rush into a relationship, and just as we may rush into a relationship with God, the verse reminds us that sustaining love takes time.

בּ:ח קוֹל דּוֹדִי הִנֵּה־זֶה בָּא מְדַלֵּג עַל־הֶהָרִים מְקַפֵּץ עַל־הַגְּבָעוֹת:

2:8 HARK! HERE COMES MY BELOVED. HE SKIPS OVER THE MOUNTAINS; HE LEAPS OVER THE HILLS.

The use of three verbs in this verse indicates the exuberance of newfound love. According to the *Targum*, when the people were enslaved in Egypt, their cry (*kol* can mean either "hark" or "a voice") ascended to the highest heavens. God then appeared to Moses at Mount Horeb and sent him to Egypt to deliver the people. The great merit of the Patriarchs (whom the author compares to mountains) and Matriarchs (whom the author compares to hills) sped the time of deliverance. Rashi also connects the verse to the events in Egypt and to the enslavement's shortened time. For Ibn Ezra, the verse is a metaphor for God's appearance to Moses at the Burning Bush and for the theophany at Sinai. Gersonides interprets the verse as a reference to the process an individual uses to attain intellectual virtue after achieving moral virtue. He reminds us to carefully follow the proper procedure of investigation to avoid being misled by imagination or by a mistake in thought, which would lead the individual away from truth and toward error. This is an example of how Gersonides uses the Song of Songs as a sort of primer for philosophy. We can use the text similarly as we try to navigate our relationship with the Divine.

ב:ט דּוֹמֶה דוֹדִי לִצְבִי אוֹ לְעֹפֶר הָאַיָּלִים הִנֵּה־זֶה עוֹמֵד אַחַר כָּתְלֵנוּ מַשְׁגִּיחַ מִן־הַחַלֹּנוֹת מֵצִיץ מִן־הַחֲרַכִּים:

2:9 MY BELOVED IS LIKE A GAZELLE OR A FAWN. THERE HE IS, STANDING BEHIND OUR WALL, LOOKING THROUGH THE WINDOWS AND PEERING THROUGH THE LATTICE.

The descriptions of a gazelle and a fawn could be the author's way of suggesting the young man's beauty or the speed with which he appears and disappears. The remainder of the verse seems like a statement that the young woman's lover is near, or that she hopes he is near.

Seeing a connection with the previous verse, the *Targum* takes this verse as a reference to Israel's response to the events of the Passover watch night. On that night, God's Presence was revealed, all the firstborn of Egypt died, and the firstborn of Israel were saved. Rashi also interprets the verse as Israel's response to being delivered from Egyptian slavery. Ibn Ezra understands "windows" as a metaphor for God looking down from heaven. For Gersonides, "the lattice" is a philosophical metaphor: the lattice allows the two lovers to see each other, yet it prevents them from making contact. Thus, for proper apprehension, one must proceed through the veil of matter to make contact with the Active Intellect.

These comments serve as reminders that we are not always able to discern God's presence in the world so clearly. Therefore, it can be difficult to establish a relationship with the Divine, a goal that appears diffuse and unclear. In seeking out a relationship with God, we are trying to achieve greater clarity.

ב:י עָנָה דוֹדִי וְאָמַר לִי קוּמִי לָךְ רַעְיָתִי יָפָתִי וּלְכִי־לָךְ:

2:10 MY BELOVED CALLED OUT TO ME: "GET UP, MY DARLING, MY BEAUTY, AND COME AWAY."

Perhaps this verse conveys part of the young woman's dream, rather than what she actually hears from her lover. The *Targum* takes the verse as the response of the Divine Lover to the people of Israel during the night in Egypt when they were told to leave. Rashi and Ibn Ezra follow the *Targum*, but Rashi claims that God's response was channeled through Moses. Gersonides understands the verse as the statement made to the intellect to proceed toward attaining the perfection yearned for. He posits that "my beauty" refers to the necessity of moral virtues as preparation for acquiring the intellectual virtues.

ב:יא כִּי־הִנֵּה הסתו הַסְּתָיו עָבָר הַגֶּשֶׁם חָלַף הָלַךְ לוֹ:

2:11 LOOK, THE WINTER IS GONE, THE RAINY SEASON IS
OVER.

This straightforward statement expresses the joys of spring. When one is in love, the world always looks like spring—beautiful and inviting. And in spring, we feel ready for a renewed relationship with God, as well. Yet, this candid reading is insufficient for the commentators, who seek to find more in the verse. According to the *Targum*, "the winter" and "the rainy season" refer to the enslavement in Egypt, which will never be experienced again. Both Rashi and Ibn Ezra follow the *Targum*. Ibn Ezra, however, explains further that the rainy season can also be a metaphor for suffering. For Gersonides, "winter" and "the rainy season" signify a different kind of darkness: the darkness of material desires versus the hope of spring. The time has come when our physical desires will not hinder the intellect's progress toward perfection.

ב:יב הַנִּצָּנִים נִרְאוּ בָאָרֶץ עֵת הַזָּמִיר הִגִּיעַ וְקוֹל הַתּוֹר נִשְׁמַע בְּאַרְצֵנוּ:

2:12 FLOWERS CAN BE SEEN IN THE LAND. THE TIME OF
SINGING HAS COME. THE SOUND OF THE TURTLEDOVE
IS HEARD IN OUR LAND.

The commentators essentially ignore the spring optimism and beauty in this verse. Rather, for the *Targum*, the "flowers" represent Moses and Aaron, who have come to Egypt to work miracles and deliver the people, just as was promised to Abraham (Genesis 15:13–14). Following the *Targum*, Rashi adds that "the time of singing" is a reference to the Song of the Sea (Exodus 15). Ibn Ezra agrees with Rashi about the Song of the Sea but feels that "flowers" refer to the righteous. He takes *tor*, the word for "turtledove," as a homonym that means "turn." Thus, it is now "Israel's turn." Gersonides, whose comment also encompasses the next verse, notes that just as there are set times when flowers bloom, when birds fly south, when fig trees produce fruit, and when vines send forth their aroma, there are also times when one should proceed toward philosophical perfection. Gersonides seems to say that we should always be ready for philosophical perfection, but we should also always be ready to intensify our relationship with the Divine. And just as spring is the right time to pursue human love, it is the right time to pursue the Divine, as well.

ב:יג הַתְּאֵנָה חָנְטָה פַגֶּיהָ וְהַגְּפָנִים סְמָדַר נָתְנוּ רֵיחַ קוּמִי לָכִי לָךְ
רַעְיָתִי יָפָתִי וּלְכִי־לָךְ:

2:13 THE FIGS ON THE FIG TREE RIPEN. THE FLOWER BUDS
OF THE VINES GIVE OFF FRAGRANCE. MY BEAUTIFUL
DARLING, ARISE AND COME AWAY.

Here is another set of images that illustrate the special time of the year for physical
and divine love. The words *chantah* (ripen) and *s'madar* (the flower buds of the vine)
are used in the Bible in this sense only here. In our translation, we have followed
Koehler-Baumgartner (pp. 333, 759). For the *Targum*, the verse refers again to the
Song of the Sea sung by the Israelites, who are compared to "ripening figs," while
their children are compared to "the flower buds on the vine." Rashi believes that the
verse refers to the entrance to the Land of Israel and to the time of the offerings of
wine. Ibn Ezra understands the verse as a reference to the first fruits of the Land, as
well as the offerings of wine.

ב:יד יוֹנָתִי בְּחַגְוֵי הַסֶּלַע בְּסֵתֶר הַמַּדְרֵגָה הַרְאִינִי אֶת־מַרְאַיִךְ
הַשְׁמִיעִינִי אֶת־קוֹלֵךְ כִּי־קוֹלֵךְ עָרֵב וּמַרְאֵיךְ נָאוֶה:

2:14 O MY DOVE, IN THE CLEFT OF THE ROCK, IN THE
HIDING PLACE IN THE CLIFF, LET ME SEE WHAT YOU
LOOK LIKE, LET ME HEAR YOUR VOICE, FOR YOUR VOICE
IS DELIGHTFUL AND YOU LOOK SO BEAUTIFUL.

At first glance, these verses read like the plot of a modern romance novel: boy finds
girl, boy loses girl, boy finds girl again. But it can also be read as a story about our
search for God: we find God, we get disillusioned, we find God once again. Like the
"dove" high up on the mountain, the young woman is out of reach but is nevertheless
nearby. So her lover calls out to her, asking that she appear to him.

The *Targum* returns to the theme of the Exodus from Egypt, suggesting that the
"dove" was pursued by a wicked Pharaoh, hemmed in on all sides (see Exodus
14:10ff. and *M'chilta*, *B'shalach* 3–4). Israel was delivered by virtue of its deeds ("you
look so beautiful") and its prayers ("your voice is delightful"). Rashi alludes to the
passage from the *M'chilta* and explains that Israel was in the same dire danger
as a dove that is pursued by a hawk. In his explanation of *madreigah* ("the cliff,"
or in other contexts "steps" or "levels"), Rashi references the Old French word
eshkaloyosh (in modern French, *escaliers*, staircases), "grooves that go around
towers." Possibly projecting his own unhappy love affair, Ibn Ezra takes the verse
literally, imagining a young man saying to the young woman, "You are hidden away in
your house, and I can't get to see you. It is as if you were a dove hidden in the cleft of
the rock. At least," he says, "stand near the lattice work and let me see you. Let me
hear your voice and tell me what to do." Gersonides reads the sights and sounds of

love as indicators that sight and hearing are the most important senses with which to begin a philosophical investigation.

בוטו אֶחֱזוּ־לָנוּ שׁוּעָלִים שׁוּעָלִים קְטַנִּים מְחַבְּלִים כְּרָמִים וּכְרָמֵינוּ
סְמָדַר:

2:15 CATCH THE FOXES FOR US, THE LITTLE FOXES ARE DESTROYING THE VINES, AND OUR VINES ARE IN BLOOM.

Although some may take this verse as a simple song sung by the young woman to her lover just so that he might hear her sweet voice, the *Targum* expresses the thought that it contains certain notions relating to events that followed the crossing of the Red Sea. No sooner had the Israelites crossed than they quarreled with Moses about water (Exodus 17:2). Since they had not followed the instructions of the Torah, and since he hated them because Jacob took from Esau both birthright and blessing, Amalek (Esau's grandson and the ultimate enemy of Israel) attacked the Israelites (Exodus 17:8). Because they worshiped idols (Judges 18:22–26), the wicked Amalek would also kill members of the tribe of Dan. They are the "foxes" whose sin tainted all Israel, who are compared to "vines." Rashi takes the verse to refer both to the events prior to the Exodus from Egypt and to the crossing of the Red Sea. "The foxes" and "the little foxes" refer to the Egyptians, young and old, who searched for newborn Israelite boys that might have been cast into the Nile. Ibn Ezra understands the verse as instructions given by the young woman to her servants who guard the vineyard where she wishes to meet her lover.

Gersonides reads the verse as an indication that there are impediments to thought other than the pleasures of the body. They are mistakes in thought, such as when we think that something accidental is essential or when we think that something exists when it does not, or vice versa. The use of logic begins the process of removing such impediments, for it directs the intellect to avoid such mistakes and begin acquiring truth. If we "catch the foxes," that is, the areas of error at the beginning, we shall have fewer mistakes at the end. The "vines...in bloom" indicate that the mistaken results, if caught early enough, can easily be corrected.

בוטז דּוֹדִי לִי וַאֲנִי לוֹ הָרֹעֶה בַּשׁוֹשַׁנִּים:

2:16 MY LOVE IS MINE AND I AM HIS, WHO GRAZES AMONG THE LILIES.

Getting as close to the literal meaning of this triumphant statement of love as he felt comfortable, Ibn Ezra takes the last clause as a reference to the couple's perfumed bower of love.

The *Targum* refers the verse to Israel's repentance, which enabled Moses—with the assistance of Joshua and Hur—to triumph over Amalek (Exodus 17:8–13). By repenting, Israel was able to reenter a relationship of love with God and thereby have the strength to conquer evil. Rashi takes the verse as a reflection of the covenant. Only from Israel (and from no other people) has God required the observance of Passover and Shavuot and the building of the Sanctuary. And only from God (and from no other deity) has Israel asked for its needs. Rashi reads "grazes among the lilies" as a symbol of a rich and fulfilling life. Ibn Ezra interprets the verse as a reference to events after the building of the Golden Calf (Exodus 32), when the wicked were destroyed and the righteous ("the lilies") were saved. Following on the previous verse, Gersonides notes that when the impediments of thought are removed, then the human intellect can be linked to the Active Intellect ("my love").

ב:יז עַד שֶׁיָּפוּחַ הַיּוֹם וְנָסוּ הַצְּלָלִים סֹב דְּמֵה־לְךָ דוֹדִי לִצְבִי אוֹ לְעֹפֶר הָאַיָּלִים עַל־הָרֵי בָתֶר:

2:17 UNTIL THE DAY COOLS DOWN AND THE SHADOWS FLEE, TURN, MY LOVE, LIKE A GAZELLE OR A FAWN ON HILLS OF PERFUME.

In the phrase *harei vater*, *vater* could be a reference to a place name (Betar). Perhaps, as Koehler-Baumgartner suggests (p. 167), on the basis of Song of Songs 4:6, *har hamor* (hill of myrrh), and 8:14, *harei v'samim* (hills of spices), and a proposed etymology related to a spice plant, it means "perfume."

The *Targum* relates the verse to God forgiving the Israelites after the sin of the Golden Calf, a theme that emerges repeatedly in the *Targum*. That sin caused the clouds of glory, which had shielded the people from the sun (during their desert journey), to depart. It caused the removal of the Israelites' armor, which was inscribed with the Divine Name and had protected them. Had it not been for the promises made to Abraham, Isaac, and Jacob (and Sarah, Rebekah, Rachel, and Leah), God would have destroyed them. God remembered how quick, like gazelles, the Patriarchs had been to offer sacrifices. God also remembered that Abraham had been willing to offer up Isaac. And God remembered the covenant made with Abraham "between the pieces," commonly known as *bein hab'tarim* (though the actual words of the Torah text are *bein hag'zarim* [Genesis 15:17–18]).

Rashi ties the verse to the incident of the Golden Calf without adding further comment, but Ibn Ezra first reads the verse literally and then interprets it figuratively. Literally, he understands it as the response of the young woman to her lover. She will not be able to go out until "the shadows flee," that is, until the days grow longer. Figuratively, it is the response of the *Shechinah*, the Presence of God, to the Israelites: following the Golden Calf incident, since God's Presence would no longer be in the camp, Moses had to pitch his tent outside the camp.

Gersonides regards the phrases "the day cools down" and "the shadows flee" as references to the night, which suggests the extreme diligence required to achieve philosophical enlightenment. The words *harei vater*, whatever their literal meaning, are understood by Gersonides to mean the various mathematical sciences that prepare us for the study of natural science. He seems to take *harei vater* as "hills of perfume,'' as we do, since, he explains, the use of such terms as *har hamor* and *harei v'samim* suggests the nature of the proofs in the natural science. In this way, "we cool down,'' so to speak, or literally, "breathe in'' from natural items. We deduce what will occur in the future from what has occurred in the past. But the science of metaphysics, Gersonides reminds us, is different. It requires the strongest kind of proof, and its notions are derived from first principles. In general, the sciences are compared to "hills'' because mastering them, like climbing hills, can be achieved only with great difficulty.

World-to-Come

The eschatological concept of a world-to-come *(olam haba)* developed during the period of the Second Temple. This concept was subsequently expanded upon in rabbinic literature. While the term *olam* was originally related to space, it later took on the dimension of time. Jewish tradition suggests that a major event, such as the Day of Judgment, would bring this world to an end and usher in the next world, that is, the world-to-come. "Heaven" and "paradise" are English terms used interchangeably to define *olam haba*. However, some make a distinction between the temporary place where souls reside prior to final judgment and the "other world" where the departed souls of "good" people reside permanently.

Tent of Meeting

The name of this tent, *Ohel Mo-eid* in Hebrew, was one of the terms used to refer to the portable desert Sanctuary that the Israelites carried with them during their travels in Sinai. On a few occasions, the Tent of Meeting was a simple structure that Moses pitched outside of the camp. While Joshua, as Moses's spiritual apprentice, remained in the Tent of Meeting at all times, Moses visited it on occasion, particularly when he wanted to engage in a dialogue with God. At these times, God "traveled" to the Tent of Meeting in the form of a cloud and met the prophet at the entrance to the tent. These meetings seemed to have occurred only to give instruction to Moses, rather than as the occasion for any worship or ritual. As a result, some commentators have argued that the Tent of Meeting and the Tabernacle were two different structures, although there is no way to be sure. Perhaps their descriptions simply emerged from different literary traditions.

Manna and Quail

Manna was the food miraculously provided by God during the Israelites' journey through the wilderness as detailed in Exodus 16:4–35. The Torah describes it as a thin layer of a seedlike substance, much like hoarfrost or coriander seed, suitable for different kinds of processing. On Fridays, the Israelites gathered a double portion of manna so that they would not have to do so on Shabbat, and it remained fresh throughout Shabbat. This is one of the bases for the custom of using two challah loaves on the Shabbat evening table. Manna ceased being provided once the Israelites crossed the Jordan River. While manna physically sustained the Israelites, it addressed their spiritual needs as well, as noted in the Torah: "in order to teach you that humans do not live on bread only, but that humans may live on anything that *Adonai* decrees" (Deuteronomy 8:3). In various places, manna is referred to as "food from heaven" (Exodus 16:4) and "heavenly grain" (Psalm 78:24).

Because the Israelites complained that the manna was becoming routine and boring, God provided them with quail to eat. But their constant complaining caused God to send them so much meat that it began to come out of their nostrils: "The meat was still between their teeth when [the people] began to die. *Adonai*'s anger was displayed against the people, and *Adonai* struck them most severely. The place of this incident was named 'Graves of Craving' *[Kivrot HaTaavah]*, since it was in that place where they buried the people who had these cravings" (Numbers 11:33–34).

Yetzer Hara, Yetzer Hatov

The Rabbis identified two complementary sets of drives that coexist in each person. One set of drives, which may be classified as libidinal drives or urges, include sex, hunger, and the like, and are grouped under the term *yetzer hara* (the inclination to evil). While these drives are not evil in themselves, left unchecked they may lead the individual to evil. For example, while the sexual drive may lead the individual to procreate, it can also lead to lust and illicit sexual behavior. The hunger drive will lead an individual to nourish the body with food but can also lead to gluttony. The *yetzer hara* is kept in balance by the *yetzer hatov* (the inclination to do good). Similarly, these drives to good must be kept in balance by the *yetzer hara*. According to this understanding, individuals who may want to give *tz'dakah*, for example, run the risk of placing themselves or their families in jeopardy should they give all of their money to charitable causes.

Satan

In the Bible, Satan is not used as a proper name, nor is it a reference to a demonic antagonist to God (except for its use in I Chronicles 21:1). Instead, Satan is an adversary —sometimes even human—that opposes and obstructs. It is also used in the context of a metaphoric court of law to refer to the prosecutor and the role of the antagonist in general. In the Book of Job, Satan is a member of the celestial court and is clearly subordinate to God. Satan is given a much more prominent role in the Talmud and midrash, where he is even identified as the *yetzer hara* (the evil inclination) and the Angel of Death (Babylonian Talmud, *Bava Batra* 16a). He appears as the tempter, but his role is more clearly defined by the Rabbis as the accuser. Reference to Satan in the liturgy is sparse, although Satan is mentioned in the *Hashkiveinu* of the evening service and the morning blessings that precede *P'sukei D'zimrah*.

The Disaster That Befell the Tribe of Ephraim

According to the midrash (*P'sikta Rabbati* 37), the tribe of Ephraim miscalculated the duration of their Egyptian bondage and left Egypt thirty years before the rest of the Israelites. As a result, the Philistines attacked them and killed 300,000 of them. Their bones were piled along the road as a warning to the rest of the Israelites not to enter the Land of Israel too soon. That is one of the reasons why God took the people on a circuitous route from Egypt through the desert on their way to Canaan. The Talmud (*Sanhedrin* 92b) suggests that it was these bones that the prophet Ezekiel revived in his "vision of the dry bones" (Ezekiel 37).

The Burning Bush

The Burning Bush is the thorn bush—which some identify as an acacia shrub—from which God spoke to Moses in the wilderness. It was from this bush that God called Moses to his prophetic mission (Exodus 3:1–10). While God's Presence appeared as a flame of fire, the "bush was not consumed" (Exodus 3:2). As a result, the Burning Bush has become a symbol of Israel.

The Theophany at Sinai

The theophany at Sinai is generally referred to as the giving of the Torah *(matan Torah),* when God was revealed to the people through Moses. According to the Torah—and Jewish tradition—this event occurred at a mountain in the Sinai desert, hence the name Mount Sinai. Regardless of whether or not one accepts that revelation took place at a specific time and place, the Sinai (or Sinaitic) experience that took place during the journey from Egypt to Canaan transformed the Jewish people.

Watch Night of Passover

On the last night that the Israelites spent in Egypt, God let loose the tenth of ten plagues against Egypt, which precipitated Pharaoh's permitting the Israelites to leave. As a response to Pharaoh's edict to kill the firstborn boys of Israel, this plague killed the firstborn of Egypt. Anticipating the visit of the Angel of Death, the Israelites smeared lamb's blood on the doorposts of their homes to distinguish them from Egyptian homes so that the angel might pass over them and not visit death upon them. This night became known as the watch night of Passover.

Song of the Sea

The Song of the Sea (*Shirat HaYam* in Hebrew) is featured prominently and graphically in the Book of Exodus (15:1–18) and is contained in the weekly portion known as *B'shalach*. When it is recited publicly, it is chanted in its own mode of cantillation. In many synagogues, the congregation rises and the Torah scroll is held aloft as it is read. The song itself, recited on the other side of the Red Sea, recounts the deliverance of Israel from the pursuing Egyptian army. It contains the well-known *Mi Chamochah*, which has become the short version of the entire song. The Rabbis were so taken by the text that they included it in its entirety in the fixed liturgy of the morning service and added to it three messianic verses from other places in the Bible. Their message was clear: just as God redeemed our people in the past, God will again redeem our people in the future.

First Fruits

The holiday of Shavuot is also called Chag HaBikurim, the Holiday of the First Fruits, recognizing the obligation of ancient Jewish farmers to bring their first fruits of the spring harvest season to the Temple. The seven species from the Land of Israel are wheat, barley, grapes, figs, pomegranates, olives, and dates. Farmers close to Jerusalem brought fresh fruits, while those who traveled from a distance generally brought dried fruits or money. Then they celebrated with the music of fifes, timbrels, and drums. The context for this requirement is found in its entirety in Deuteronomy 26:1–11, the centerpiece of which is verses 1–2: "When you come into the Land that *Adonai* your God is giving you as an inheritance, and you possess it and begin to take permanent residence in it, then you shall take all the fruit of the ground, which you shall bring from your Land that *Adonai* your God is giving you. You shall put it in a basket, and you shall go to the place that *Adonai* your God will choose as a residence for the Divine Name." The procedure for what one is do to with the fruits is contained in the Mishnah (*Bikurim* 3:3–4).

Covenant between the Pieces

God's first covenant with Abraham, who is still called Abram at the time, is referred to as the "covenant between the pieces." It is a reference to the flame torch that passed through the pieces of a sacrifice (in Genesis 15:17–18). According to scholars, this was a common ancient Near Eastern method for "cutting a deal." Jeremiah 34:17–18 reminds us that if the agreement is broken by the junior partner, then that person ends up symbolically "cut into pieces." This covenant resulted from Abram's request for a guarantee from God that his descendants would inherit the Land of Israel. God makes this graphic covenant because Abram keeps asking, "How will I know?" The Torah text is powerful and uplifting: "Do not fear, Abram, I am a shield to you. Your reward will be very great" (Genesis 15:1). But these words are insufficient for Abram, and he presses God for a guarantee. The textual context of this covenant in Genesis (15:7–21) outlines the borders of the Land and emphasizes the sacrifices and divine fire that accompanied the pact. In anticipation of this covenantal agreement, God caused Abram to fall into a deep sleep. In the dreaded darkness of the night, Abram is told of the people's destiny.

The nighttime vision reaches into the depths of his soul. According to Robert Alter, this nighttime experience implies a "prophetic mode of experience" (*Genesis: Translation and Commentary*, p. 63). Rabbi Joseph Soloveitchik (in *The Voice of My Beloved Knocks*) refers to this covenant as "our national covenant of fate." Such a covenant is imposed on the individual; it is not chosen.

God's Use of Nations of the World

According to the rabbinic understanding of God's ways, God uses the nations of the world to act against the people of Israel, particularly when God has determined that they have acted contrary to divine directives and have transgressed. While God may have acted directly to flood the world in the early chapters of the Bible, many later punishments are meted out at the hands of others. The Reform Movement has rejected much of this theology, although traditional Judaism views the destruction of the Temple and the dispersion from the Land as a direct result of God's intervention: God punished the people for their behavior.

GLEANINGS

The Jewish Pleasure Principle

There is a *reality principle* that is associated with the Jewish *pleasure principle*. That reality principle affirms that for pleasure to be of ennobling quality, it must be a meaningful pleasure, experienced in a meaningful context. In Talmudic terms, this translates as pleasure associated with the fulfillment of a commandment. This is real pleasure, rather than intoxicating pleasure, pleasure that comes from an authentic life joy, experienced in sobriety, that can be recalled the day after.

Moreover, because it is a pleasure associated with *reasons* rather than with *causes*, it is more likely to be a pleasure that is a *plateau* rather than a *peak*. Pleasure as a "high" is apt to be a sudden but transient episode in an otherwise featureless existence, a peak that is surely to be followed by a valley or a hangover.

On the other hand, pleasure that is real and meaningful is that which has enduring and positive aftereffects. The person who is pleased at having performed a good deed, at having helped someone else, is not likely to rest on his [or her] laurels or to see that performance as a rationale for not helping anyone else in the future. At the same time, that feeling of having pleased someone else and done something beneficial leaves the doer in a pleased state—happy, if not ecstatic, at having been able to help, and at the same time eager to do further good deeds when the opportunity arises, even seeking such opportunities.

Reuven Bulka, *Judaism on Pleasure* (Northvale, NJ: Jason Aronson, 1995), 78–79

Matzah, the Food of the Watch Night

Matzah is part of the first Passover. On their last night in Egypt, in the terror of a final watch night of not knowing, Jewish families gathered in their homes and celebrated a first Seder. This was the night of the tenth plague, the night that death would visit every Egyptian home. It was a night of death and terror. To keep their homes safe, each family had dipped a hyssop plant in the blood of a lamb and painted its *mezuzot*, doorposts. That night, gathered inside, they ate this Pesach lamb just as God had ordered Moses to tell them, "with matzah and maror (bitter herbs) shall you eat it." Matzah is the food of the Seder celebration. Its taste connects every Seder to our Seder, every telling of the Exodus to our telling.

Joel Lurie Grishaver, *Building Jewish Life: Passover Activity Book*
(Los Angeles: Torah Aura Productions, 1988), 44

The Song at the Sea

But Israel knew that beyond history and revealing itself within it, there dwells the great patience. World history has become patient justice.... Revenge is reserved for God.... The people remained faithful to this song and to this belief and with it history itself became a song. History was not only an apprehension and a narration of that which had happened here; nor was it only a possession of these who pursued this knowledge and power. It lived within the people as its certainty. History was interwoven with that day which came and which was to come.

This people is in fact a singing people.... Every day desires its song; even the darkness must have it.

Leo Baeck, *This People Israel: The Meaning of Jewish Existence*
(Philadelphia: Jewish Publication Society, 1965), 37–38, 40

God Dwells in the Presence of Love

The world can be a very harsh and lonely place sometimes. It is love, more than anything else, that helps us break down the prison of isolation we feel. Both the love we give and the love we receive. For what is love but a willingness to extend beyond ourselves, to take risks, to be there for another, and to trust that the other will be there for us.

The loving relationship is so ecstatic because it is the human epitome of the yearning for oneness that pervades the entire cosmos. That is what we mean when we say the prayer known as the *Sh'ma*. We say that God is One. Everything in the world hungers for unity. God is the ultimate unity. The ultimate oneness. When we love without ulterior motives, when we love wholeheartedly, when the boundaries of self disappear, for that moment we achieve a oneness with the other, the world, and with everything around us. We overcome our loneliness through conscious acts of loving. God dwells in the presence of such love.

Terry Bookman, *The Busy Soul: Ten-Minute Spiritual Workouts Drawn from Jewish Tradition*
(New York: Perigee, 1999), 112–13

CHAPTER THREE

ג:א עַל־מִשְׁכָּבִי בַּלֵּילוֹת בִּקַּשְׁתִּי אֵת שֶׁאָהֲבָה נַפְשִׁי בִּקַּשְׁתִּיו וְלֹא
מְצָאתִיו:

3:1 ON MY BED AT NIGHT, I SOUGHT THE ONE I LOVE.
I SOUGHT HIM, BUT I COULD NOT FIND HIM.

Either the young woman is expressing her yearning for her lover to others or she is
speaking to herself in a dream.

The *Targum* suggests that the verse is a metaphor for the results of the sin of the
Golden Calf. The clouds of glory were taken from the Israelites, and it seemed as if
darkness had descended upon them. The crown of holiness, which they had received
at Mount Sinai, was also taken from them. Although they looked for it, they couldn't
find it.

Rashi notes that the Golden Calf incident caused the Israelites to be out of favor
with God for thirty-eight years. God withdrew the Divine Presence from among them.
Ibn Ezra also relates this verse to the events surrounding the sin of the Golden Calf.
In his reading, the phrase "on my bed" indicates illness, not desire. "At night"
suggests that the people of Israel were in a state of spiritual darkness. "I sought him"
shows that the Israelites yearned for God to be in their midst. In Gersonides's reading,
the phrase "at night" instead implies a darkness of ignorance, while "I sought him"
suggests the yearning for ultimate perfection. Further, "I could not find him" reminds
us that we cannot achieve the goal of ultimate perfection without proceeding in
the proper order.

ג:ב אָקוּמָה נָּא וַאֲסוֹבְבָה בָעִיר בַּשְּׁוָקִים וּבָרְחֹבוֹת אֲבַקְשָׁה אֵת
שֶׁאָהֲבָה נַפְשִׁי בִּקַּשְׁתִּיו וְלֹא מְצָאתִיו:

3:2 I MUST GET UP AND GO AROUND THE CITY. IN THE
MARKETS AND IN THE STREETS, I WILL SEEK THE ONE
I LOVE. I SOUGHT HIM, BUT I COULD NOT FIND HIM.

The words *sh'vakim* and *r'chovot* present an interesting challenge of translation,
precisely because their meanings seem familiar and synonymous. Both can mean
"street," but they probably reflect different stages in the development of cities.
The singular of *sh'vakim* is *shuk*, a marketplace—so named because business was
often carried out in the street. The singular of *r'chovot* is *r'chov*. While in Modern
Hebrew *r'chov* is generally translated as "street," its etymology and its ancient usage

imply a broad and open space (see Genesis 19:2), what we might today call a "plaza" or "square."

The *Targum* evidently had the same problem of distinguishing *sh'vakim* from *r'chovot*, since its translation employs the Greek loan words *f'lataya* (wide streets, broad places, highways) for the first and *fatvan* (wide open places) for the second. Interestingly, in the *Targum's* metaphoric interpretation of the verse, it uses *nischar* (let us go about), as if there is more than one person involved. The root of the word *s'char*, which means to go about as a merchant, is related to *s'chorah*, the Hebrew word for "business." The *Targum* explains that the chastened Israelites are looking to find Moses, in order to get divine instruction so that the *Shechinah* might once again dwell in their midst. But they cannot find Moses. Rashi refers the verse to the words of Moses, who seeks atonement for the people (Exodus 32:30).

ג:ג מְצָאוּנִי הַשֹּׁמְרִים הַסֹּבְבִים בָּעִיר אֵת שֶׁאָהֲבָה נַפְשִׁי רְאִיתֶם:

3:3 THE GUARDS WHO PATROL THE CITY FOUND ME. [I ASKED,] "HAVE YOU SEEN THE ONE I LOVE?"

While it is still not clear whether this is a real event or a dream, the verse tells of a young woman who has gone out at night. There is a sense that the "markets" or "streets" are dangerous at night, either because they are filled with people or because they are empty. "The guards" could suggest that it is late at night and the places, once crowded, are now empty. In such a setting nameless danger lurks, and the guards have come upon the solitary and lonely young woman.

For the *Targum*, "the guards" signify Moses, Aaron, and the Levites. The Israelites have turned to them, asking where the *Shechinah* has gone. Moses responds, "To heaven," and adds that he will ascend to the highest heaven to pray for the people. Perhaps God will grant atonement for their sins and will once again allow the Divine Presence to dwell in their midst. Rashi also thinks that "the guards" refers to Moses and Aaron. "Have you seen" is understood by him as "What have you heard him say?" Taking the verse literally, Ibn Ezra thinks that this is part of the young woman's dream. On a figurative level, he agrees with the interpretation of Rashi and the *Targum*. For Gersonides, the "guards" are the senses. They help preserve every kind of animal. However, the senses can mislead us when their impressions are mingled in the mind.

ג:ד כִּמְעַט שֶׁעָבַרְתִּי מֵהֶם עַד שֶׁמָּצָאתִי אֵת שֶׁאָהֲבָה נַפְשִׁי אֲחַזְתִּיו
וְלֹא אַרְפֶּנּוּ עַד־שֶׁהֲבֵיאתִיו אֶל־בֵּית אִמִּי וְאֶל־חֶדֶר הוֹרָתִי:

3:4 NO SOONER HAD I PASSED THEM WHEN I FOUND THE
ONE THAT I LOVE. I GRABBED HIM AND WOULD NOT
LET HIM GO UNTIL I BROUGHT HIM TO MY MOTHER'S
HOUSE, TO THE ROOM OF THE ONE WHO HAD
CONCEIVED ME.

Perhaps this is a retelling of events by the young woman or a reflection of her desires. However, the *Targum* argues that it is an illustration of God's anger. God instructed Moses to set up the Tent of Meeting so that the Divine Presence might rest there. The Israelites would bring their sacrifices there and study Torah at its entrance with Moses, their teacher, and his servant Joshua. Since Rashi understands "the guards" to be Moses and Aaron, he takes "no sooner had I passed them" as Israel's lament on their leaders' deaths, because they had led the people through the wilderness for forty years. "I found the one" is a reference to God, who was with the people when Joshua fought the battle of the thirty-one kings (Joshua 12:1–24).

ג:ה הִשְׁבַּעְתִּי אֶתְכֶם בְּנוֹת יְרוּשָׁלַם בִּצְבָאוֹת אוֹ בְּאַיְלוֹת הַשָּׂדֶה
אִם־תָּעִירוּ וְאִם־תְּעוֹרְרוּ אֶת־הָאַהֲבָה עַד שֶׁתֶּחְפָּץ:

3:5 O DAUGHTERS OF JERUSALEM, I CHARGE YOU, BY THE
ROES OR THE HINDS OF THE FIELD: DON'T WAKE,
DON'T EXCITE LOVE UNTIL IT PLEASES.

While this verse is a repetition of 2:7, the *Targum* reads new meaning into it and adds its own dialogue. When the seven nations residing in Canaan heard that the Israelites would inherit their land in the future, they arose as one and cut down all the trees, stopped up the wells, destroyed the towns, and drove out all the inhabitants. As a result, God said to Moses, "I took an oath to your ancestors that I would bring their children to possess a land flowing with milk and honey. How then could I bring their children to an empty and desolate land? Therefore, I will keep you in the wilderness for forty years so that my Torah will be absorbed into your bodies. In the interim, those nations will rebuild all that they destroyed." Moses then said to the Israelites, "O congregation of Israel, I charge you by the Lord of Hosts and by the mighty of the Land of Israel that you not plan on entering the Land of Canaan until the end of the forty years. May it be God's will that the inhabitants of the Land be delivered into your hands and that you may be able to cross the Jordan River and that you conquer the Land." Rashi reads the verse as a reference to the Babylonian exile. He takes "don't excite love" as an appeal to Israel not to be distracted or seduced away from God. "Until it pleases" suggests that God's love is still with us.

ג:ו מִי זֹאת עֹלָה מִן־הַמִּדְבָּר כְּתִימֲרוֹת עָשָׁן מְקֻטֶּרֶת מוֹר וּלְבוֹנָה מִכֹּל אַבְקַת רוֹכֵל:

3:6 WHO IS THIS COMING UP FROM THE WILDERNESS, LIKE COLUMNS OF SMOKE, PERFUMED WITH MYRRH AND FRANKINCENSE, WITH ALL THE PERFUMED POWDERS OF THE MERCHANT?

It is not clear at all to whom "who is this coming" refers. Since *olah* is a feminine participle, one might think it refers to the young woman. On reading the next verse, however, it appears that it might refer to *mitato shelish'lomo* (Solomon's litter) since *mitah* is a feminine noun. If the verb refers to the young woman, then the writer is presenting us with a change of scene, from the city to the wilderness, and from the wilderness to the city, as well as a change of voice.

The *Targum* connects the verse to the responses of the people of Canaan when they saw the Israelites enter, led by Joshua. They said, "Look at the chosen people perfumed by the incense of spices and supported by the merit of their ancestors; of Abraham, who worshiped at Moriah; of Isaac, who was willing to be bound as an offering on that mountain destined to be the place of the Temple; and of Jacob, who wrestled with an angel until dawn and then triumphed. As a result, he was delivered, as were the twelve tribes." Rashi sees the verse as a response of the Israelites who wandered the desert, directed by a pillar of cloud during the day and a pillar of fire at night. Ibn Ezra sheds light on the unusual words used in the verse by explaining that *timarot* has the same meaning as the more common *amudim* (columns), and *rocheil* has the same meaning as the more common *socheir* (merchant).

ג:ז הִנֵּה מִטָּתוֹ שֶׁלִּשְׁלֹמֹה שִׁשִּׁים גִּבֹּרִים סָבִיב לָהּ מִגִּבֹּרֵי יִשְׂרָאֵל:

3:7 HERE COMES SOLOMON'S LITTER, SIXTY WARRIORS SURROUND IT, [SIXTY] OF THE WARRIORS OF ISRAEL.

Mitato (his litter) is usually translated as "his bed." In this context, it describes a covered couch carried by servants that was a means of transportation used in the ancient world. Such a conveyance would have been available only to the upper echelons of society. Not only did it require someone to make the couch and a buyer with the means to purchase it, but it also required numerous servants or slaves to carry it.

The *Targum* explains the verse as God's response to the Temple built by Solomon: how beautiful is the building; how wonderful are the priests who stand on the platform *(duchan)* and bless the people. Their blessing acts like a wall protecting them and enables the warriors of the people to be victorious. Rashi suggests that the verse refers to the Ark and the Tent of Meeting used in the wilderness. The "sixty warriors" is an allusion to the 600,000 Israelites who surrounded the Tent of Meeting. "Of the warriors of Israel" refers to those enlisted in the ranks. Reading the verse literally, Ibn Ezra notes that a sovereign ruler would naturally require a large retinue as guards.

37

גּ:ח כֻּלָּם אֲחֻזֵי חֶרֶב מְלֻמְּדֵי מִלְחָמָה אִישׁ חַרְבּוֹ עַל־יְרֵכוֹ מִפַּחַד
בַּלֵּילוֹת:

3:8 ALL OF THEM ARMED WITH SWORDS, TRAINED IN
WARFARE, EACH WITH HIS SWORD ON HIS THIGH,
BECAUSE OF THE TERROR OF THE NIGHT.

Large open spaces are particularly dangerous at night. Even a sovereign ruler requires protection when traveling through them. For the *Targum*, the weapons that provide protection are the words of Torah preserved by the priests, the Levites, and all of the tribes of Israel. For Rashi, "warfare" is the battle for Torah. The "sword" is the Masorah, the biblical tradition that establishes the correct text for reading the Torah. And "terror of the night" is the fear of forgetting the words of Torah. Ibn Ezra considers "the terror of the night" to be fear of bandits who might kidnap the young woman venturing out into the wilderness alone. Figuratively, he considers her as the congregation of Israel. "Solomon's litter" (3:7) is the Land of Israel, and "terror of the night" is the fear of exile.

גּ:ט אַפִּרְיוֹן עָשָׂה לוֹ הַמֶּלֶךְ שְׁלֹמֹה מֵעֲצֵי הַלְּבָנוֹן:

3:9 KING SOLOMON MADE A PALANQUIN FOR HIM FROM
THE WOOD OF LEBANON.

Koehler-Baumgartner (p. 80) offers us a number of options for the derivation of the word *apiryon*, translated as "palanquin," a covered litter carried on poles on the shoulders of four or more bearers. Determining the specific derivation of the word also helps in dating *Shir HaShirim*. If *apiryon* is derived from the Greek word *aphorion*, also meaning "palanquin," then the Song of Songs could not have been composed earlier than the area's contact with Greek culture, that is, not earlier than the conquest of the area by Alexander in 311 B.C.E. However, if the word is derived from the Sanskrit *parliyamka*, then an earlier date is quite possible, because the Sanskrit word predates the Greek word. Since we have no clear indication of the trading routes in the ancient world, it is possible that there was contact with the Greek world prior to Alexander's conquest.

The *Targum* takes *apiryon* to refer to the Temple that Solomon built and specifies the kind of "wood of Lebanon": ginger, teak, and cedar. Rashi refers the word to the Tent of Meeting that would later be set in the Sanctuary at Shiloh, while Ibn Ezra indicates that in this context the word means some kind of grand building. Gersonides thinks that the word suggests the place where a marriage is consummated (the nuptial bower), which is built as a place of beauty.

ג:י עַמּוּדָיו עָשָׂה כֶסֶף רְפִידָתוֹ זָהָב מֶרְכָּבוֹ אַרְגָּמָן תּוֹכוֹ רָצוּף אַהֲבָה מִבְּנוֹת יְרוּשָׁלָם:

3:10 HE MADE ITS PILLARS OF SILVER, ITS BACK OF GOLD, ITS SEAT OF PURPLE CLOTH. ITS INTERIOR WAS LOVINGLY DECORATED BY THE DAUGHTERS OF JERUSALEM.

This simple verse presents us with some complex challenges. The word *r'fidato* (its back) occurs only here in the Bible; thus, we have translated it by context. *Ratzuf* (decorated, bedecked) is translated by Koehler-Baumgarten (p. 1285) as "inlaid," since its root meaning is "to lay firmly" or "to layer." Such a translation implies an emendation of the text from *ahavah* (lovingly) to *avanim* (precious stones, jewels), taking the *m* from *mibnot* (by the daughters). This changes *mibnot* to the vocative form, *b'not* (O daughters of Jerusalem). Thus, the last clause would read: "Its interior inlaid with jewels, O daughters of Jerusalem."

The *Targum* takes "its pillars" to refer to the Ark of the Testimony, which supports the world, and adds its own descriptions. The Ark contains the two tablets of the Law, more precious than refined silver and pure gold, and it is covered by a curtain of blue and purple cloth. Above the Ark cover stand two cherubim. The Eternal God who sets the Divine Name on Jerusalem causes the Divine Presence, the *Shechinah*, to rest on it. Rashi takes *r'fidato* as a reference to the Ark cover and the "seat" as a reference to the curtain. "Its interior...lovingly decorated" is understood by Rashi to refer to all the items, including the Ark, the Ark cover, the cherubim, and the tablets. Ibn Ezra takes *apiryon* to refer to the Temple, *r'fidato* to refer to a wing of the Temple, "seat" to refer to the basement of the Temple, which conceals the pillars, and "decorated" to refer to the brickwork in the Temple floor. Gersonides takes the opportunity to remind his readers that "daughters of Jerusalem" indicates all the capacities of the soul, which are subservient to the intellect.

ג:יא צְאֶינָה וּרְאֶינָה בְּנוֹת צִיּוֹן בַּמֶּלֶךְ שְׁלֹמֹה בָּעֲטָרָה שֶׁעִטְּרָה-לּוֹ אִמּוֹ בְּיוֹם חֲתֻנָּתוֹ וּבְיוֹם שִׂמְחַת לִבּוֹ:

3:11 COME OUT AND LOOK, O DAUGHTERS OF ZION, AT KING SOLOMON, WHO WEARS THE CROWN WITH WHICH HIS MOTHER CROWNED HIM ON HIS WEDDING DAY, ON THE DAY THAT HIS HEART REJOICED.

Although *tz'enah* could be translated as "go out," the idiomatic sense of the verse suggests "come out," since the young women are being asked to "come out" of their houses. It is not immediately clear whether this is a reference to the historical event of Solomon's wedding where Bathsheba was to present a crown to her son, apparently a standard wedding ritual during which the groom plays a royal part and is "crowned." The Mishnah (*Sotah* 9:14) recounts such a practice.

The *Targum* applies this verse to the scene at the dedication of the Temple, seeing the verse as a proclamation that all those who lived in the Land of Israel should come and see the crown and wreath with which the people of Israel crowned King Solomon. In response to the intense joy of the people, Solomon declared that the celebration would last fourteen days. Changing the context and character of the verse completely, Rashi reads *b'not Tziyon* (daughters of Zion) not as women but as "sons who are distinguished *(m'tzuyanim)* to God by the specific mitzvot of *b'rit milah, t'fillin,* and *tzitzit.*" Then he takes "the crown" as a reference to the Tent of Meeting, which was crowned with a cloth of blue, purple, and scarlet. Nevertheless, Rashi reads "on his wedding day" as an allusion to the day the Torah was given and "the day that his heart rejoiced" as a reference to the time that the Tabernacle was dedicated in the wilderness. Ibn Ezra connects this verse to 3:10, reading *ratzuf ahavah* (which we translated as "lovingly decorated") as *saruf ahavah* (burnt by love, infatuated). Because Solomon was infatuated by one of the *b'not Y'rushalayim* (daughters of Jerusalem), he put the "crown" (from this verse) on his head as a way of expressing his desire. Gersonides reads the verse as a reference to the soul and its capacities. For him, "his mother" refers to imaginary images that are a stage in the acquisition of ideas and the perfection of the intellect. "On the day his heart rejoiced" is, in this interpretation, a reference to the intellect's great delight and joy when it achieves perfection through the acquisition of ideas.

Crown of Holiness

A crown of holiness is not a real object and is used as a metaphor by the Rabbis: God placed the divine crown of holiness on the people of Israel as part of the covenantal relationship. Similarly, in Leviticus (see chapter 8), the prophet invests the priest with a crown of holiness. This is a metaphysical act that is accompanied by the wearing of "holy" garments by the priest after his body has been ritually washed.

Battle of Thirty-one Kings

According to the Book of Joshua, the people camped at Shittim, where Joshua assumed command of the armies of Israel. After crossing the Jordan, the Israelites made camp at Gilgal. Under the leadership of Joshua, the Israelites conquered the Land of Israel by battling six nations and thirty-one kings. After successfully assuming possession of the land from the Canaanites, Joshua divided the land among the tribes (Joshua 12:1–24).

Seven Nations

Jewish tradition suggests that seven nations (as they are referred to in the Torah) resided in the land of Canaan prior to its conquest by the Israelites. These are the Hittites, Girgashites, Emorites, Canaanites, Perizzites, Hivites, and Jebusites.

Babylonian Exile

Following the destruction of the First Temple and the conquest of Judah by Nebuchadnezzar in the year 586 B.C.E., the Israelites were forced into exile in Babylonia until 538 B.C.E., when Cyrus of Persia, the new conqueror of Babylonia, allowed them to return. This period saw the beginning of the Jewish people's Diaspora, even though many returned to the Land of Israel. There are those who believe that many of the institutions, such as the synagogue, that have sustained the Jewish people throughout the ages emerged during the Babylonian exile.

Chosen People

The notion of a chosen people, which is a central tenet of Jewish tradition, suggests that the Jewish people were chosen by God, as evidenced by the giving of the Torah. This idea is sometimes referred to as the election of Israel. While the Reform Movement has struggled with the idea of a chosen people—primarily because it is predicated on the divine revelation of Torah—the Reconstructionist Movement and its founder, Rabbi Mordecai Kaplan, rejected the notion of a chosen people outright. As a result, much of the classic liturgy, which includes formulas that reflect this idea, has been changed in Reconstructionist liturgy. For example, the standard Torah blessing includes the phrase *bachar banu mikol ha-amim*, "who has chosen us from among the peoples." This concept, which is retained in Reform liturgy, is worded in the classic Reconstructionist *siddur* instead as "who has brought us close *[keirvanu]* to Your [literally 'His'] service."

Masorah

The term "Masorah" refers to what is known as "the inherited tradition." The work of transmitting the Torah was placed in the hands of scribes. They eventually became known as transcribers who were skilled in the exact copying of the text from one scroll to another. As a result, they were knowledgeable in Torah. The primary interest of the scribes was to maintain the text of the Torah. They are, therefore, credited with a series of rules and regulations concerning the text of the Torah. Since they could not change the text, they transmitted much of their work, such as vowels and cantillation marks, orally.

Sanctuary at Shiloh

Under the leadership of Joshua (18:1), the Tabernacle was erected at Shiloh, the capital of Israel at the time of the judges. As a result, it became the center of Israelite worship.

The Ark of the Testimony

While there are a variety of terms used in Jewish tradition and in sacred literature to refer to the Ark of the Testimony, it is the compartment that housed the tablets of the covenant. Bezalel constructed the Ark according to Moses's instructions (see Exodus 25:10–22; 37:1–9). The opening at the top of the Ark was closed off by the Ark cover, at the ends of which two golden cherubim (winged celestial beings of some sort) guarded or protected it.

GLEANINGS

Your Love Lifts Me

Love is always greater than our limited ability to anticipate, because it is part of something vastly greater than we can comprehend. In our petty presumption, we think we have mastered ourselves and our feelings, but we are made in God's image, and our ability to love is our reflection of God's great love.

Out of God's boundless love, God created a world of beauty and marvel. And God fashioned a creature in that world who could share the excitement and responsibility of creative love. We love each other as an expression of God's love. God loves through us, and we love God, in part, by loving each other.

Rather than seeing our ability to love creation and other people as somehow competing with our ability to love God, I'd rather see our love with God as the base upon which our other loves thrive. A child eventually grows to be a good spouse by learning to love his or her mother and father first, so that all loves are reenactments and permutations of that earliest love. We recycle and refashion that same old love throughout our lives.

That recycling means that all our loves are connected to each other, and all are mutually reinforcing. Knowing that we can love and trust a spouse strengthens our love and trust in God—and vice versa. Learning to value and to cherish ourselves can permit us to recognize God's unconditional love for us as we are.

Learn to love freely. By loving ourselves, our spouse, our children, our parents, our community, our people, our planet, we surprise ourselves by experiencing the transforming power of love beyond our fondest hopes. And all that love can connect us to the wondrous, surprising love of the One who gave us life: God.

Bradley Shavit Artson, "Your Love Lifts Me," in *Sacred Intentions: Daily Inspiration to Strengthen the Spirit, Based on Jewish Wisdom*, ed. Kerry Olitzky and Lori Forman (Woodstock, VT: Jewish Lights, 1999), 18

Love and Marriage

Conventional Wisdom in contemporary U.S. culture is that we will meet a marriage partner through random chance and we will somehow fall in love. Little girls grow into women who still believe the fairy-tale message, "Someday my prince will come." Men believe in the classic Beatles tune *I Saw Her Standing There* and that they will someday see a woman and know she is "the one." Men and women both believe that this magic called love will carry them through fifty years of successful marriage.

In truth, love alone is not enough. Finding the right marriage partner means making wise choices. It means using one's head, not simply one's heart.

The most important ingredient for a successful marriage is trust, not love. We find someone whose values we share, who has a similar vision of the kind of home they want to build, who attracts us, who makes us feel good about ourselves. Slowly we lower our protective coverings and open our real selves to that individual. This is the purpose of courtship, to use a rather old-fashioned term. Courtship is an attempt to truly know another individual, to gradually uncover our real selves, to open up, to see if we can trust another, to become, as the Bible says of Adam and Eve, "Naked but not ashamed" (Genesis 2:25). The nakedness is not a physical nakedness but a spiritual nakedness, a willingness to allow ourselves to be vulnerable to another. This is the beginning of intimacy.

Michael Gold, *The Ten Journeys of Life: Walking the Path of Abraham*
(Deerfield Beach, FL: Simcha Press, 2001), 61–62

The Romance of God and Man

The romance of human loving is a romance made up of both unconditional and conditional love. Because they are often difficult to separate out, perhaps it would be helpful to see an extraordinary paradigm of this love, the Biblical love of God and man.

God chooses the People of Israel. That is a romance that begins for no reason that is apparent. Because God loves Israel, He gets involved with her.

Just think about it. He doesn't have to. The God of Aristotle, for example, was a God who deigned to contemplate a perfect object. Since there is only one perfect object, and that is God, Aristotle's God ended up contemplating Himself. The God of the Bible, on the other hand, decides, for better or worse, for richer or poorer, to throw in His lot with an imperfect object—with the people of Israel.

And it is exactly because He is God and because, therefore, He doesn't have to love anybody else, that His love is so important and palpable. It is a grand romance. When the prophet Jeremiah pictures God looking back on this romance He, God, thinks of it in terms of the romance of their youth. "I remember for thee the affection of thy youth, the love of thine espousals; how thou wentest after Me in the wilderness, in a land that was not sown" (Jeremiah 2:2).

Harlan J. Wechsler, *What's So Bad About Guilt?* (New York: Simon and Schuster, 1990), 173–74

Jewish Spirituality: The Way of Love

Spirituality is not theology or history or liturgy or rabbinic codes. Spirituality is our relationship to God, with all its ups and downs, engagements and withdrawals. To deepen and strengthen this relationship, we make use of the insights we gain through our theology and through our understanding of Jewish history. When we want to be in communication with God, we use our established forms of liturgy and look to the guidance of our codes. But all of these are only the instruments we use in our quest to develop our relationship. We may build a house, but it remains only a structure and does not become a home without the love of the people who reside there. We can discover something, but it becomes a treasure only when we value it. And we can structure a relationship with God, but it becomes fruitful only when we imbue it with our love.

Most Jewish prayers are written in the plural, but our love for God must be an individual experience. When we enter into marriage, the words we use to describe our relationship have been formed by the community. Our expectations for marriage are socially constructed. The marriage ceremony is codified by our faith. And yet, when we go home, close the door, and begin our day-to-day lives, the actual relationship with our spouse is individual and deeply personal. Our relationship to God is no less formed by the stories that have shaped our faith, described our history, and given form to our experiences. But while much of our relationship is expressed communally, it remains essentially individual and personal.

Carol Ochs, "Jewish Spirituality: The Way of Love," in *Paths of Faithfulness: Personal Essays on Jewish Spirituality,"* ed. Carol Ochs, Kerry M. Olitzky, and Joshua Saltzman (Hoboken, NJ: KTAV, 1997), 103–4

CHAPTER FOUR

ד:א הִנָּךְ יָפָה רַעְיָתִי הִנָּךְ יָפָה עֵינַיִךְ יוֹנִים מִבַּעַד לְצַמָּתֵךְ שַׂעְרֵךְ
כְּעֵדֶר הָעִזִּים שֶׁגָּלְשׁוּ מֵהַר גִּלְעָד:

4:1 OH, YOU ARE BEAUTIFUL, MY DARLING, YOU ARE
BEAUTIFUL. YOUR EYES ARE LIKE DOVES BEHIND YOUR
VEIL. YOUR HAIR IS LIKE A FLOCK OF GOATS BOUNDING
DOWN MOUNT GILEAD.

This verse begins with the same words as 1:15. Ostensibly, this is a description of a young woman whose face is hidden modestly behind a veil, only her "eyes like doves" visible. Yet, her hair, too, which in many cultures would also be hidden, is visible. The image of "goats bounding down" suggests that the woman has luxurious, wavy hair.

The *Targum* continues its translation/commentary by describing the dedication of the Temple, during which Solomon placed 1,000 offerings on the altar that were favorably accepted by God. A divine voice (*bat kol* in Hebrew; *bat kala* in Aramaic) went forth and proclaimed, "How beautiful are you, O congregation of Israel. How marvelous are your leaders, the Sages who form the Sanhedrin, who always enlighten the House of Israel and who may be compared to doves. The remainder of the House of Israel are righteous, even those who are unlearned. They may be compared to the monument that their ancestor Jacob made, gathering stones at Mount Gilead (Genesis 31:46–48)." Rashi also understands this verse as a reference to the Temple and the sacrifices that were made there. Since doves are known to remain true to each other even at the point of death, they are symbolic of the mutual devotion of God and the people. The veil, meanwhile, symbolizes the separation of Israel from other peoples. Following the *Targum*, Rashi relates "the flock of goats," to Jacob and his sons and their confrontation with Laban. Ibn Ezra explains *shegalshu* (bounding) in a literal manner as "visible," "frozen," or "white." This refers to the appearance of the goats themselves, rather than a description of their movement down the mountain. However, he interprets "eyes" figuratively as a reference to the prophets, who are the "eyes" of the community.

45

ד:ב שִׁנַּיִךְ כְּעֵדֶר הַקְּצוּבוֹת שֶׁעָלוּ מִן־הָרַחְצָה שֶׁכֻּלָּם מַתְאִימוֹת וְשַׁכֻּלָה אֵין בָּהֶם:

4:2 YOUR TEETH ARE LIKE A FLOCK OF NEWLY SHORN SHEEP COMING UP FROM THE WASHING POOL. ALL ARE PAIRED, AND NONE IS MISSING.

Not only does the comparison between sheep and teeth seem rather strange, but the text is not even very clear. The verb *katzav* may mean "to shape," "to butcher," or "to cut." Koehler-Baumgartner (p. 1119) takes *k'tzuvot* as "newly shorn sheep" and *mat-imot* as "to bear twins." We have followed the first translation, but not the second one. Comparing teeth to sheep that bear twins makes little sense. *Mat-im* comes to mean "parallel" or "paired" in later Hebrew. If we take *mat-imot* as "paired," then the context demands that we translate *shakulah* (she who loses a child) as "missing."

For the *Targum*, "teeth" seems to suggest a reference to the praiseworthy priests and Levites who offer the sacrifices and eat them, receiving freely offered tithes and heave offerings. Their virtue reminds the commentator of one of Jacob's newly shorn flocks as it emerges from a stream. The sheep all look alike; they come in twin pairs; none miscarries. Rashi interprets this verse literally. He takes the description of the teeth as a general characterization of the woman's beauty. Her teeth are small, white, and perfectly ordered, like a choice flock of ewes given to a skilled shepherd to tend. Such animals produce high-quality wool to make fine garments. Hence, they are carefully watched and washed daily in order to protect the wool. Rashi does not read *mat-imot* as twins; rather, he takes it as a plural of *m'tom* (healthy parts), as found in Psalm 38:4 and 38:8. He takes *shakulah* to be derived from *shakul* (bereaved of a child), a synonym of *mum* (blemish), thus, understanding the last phrase of the verse as "all of them are healthy, and none are blemished." Rashi then takes the entire passage as a parable that describes the heroes of Israel, who are free of any transgression and are not suspected of theft or sexual improprieties, but who consume their enemies. They are the warriors who defeated the Midianites (Numbers 31:49ff.), yet they took nothing of the spoil for themselves. Ibn Ezra reads *k'tzuvot* (newly shorn sheep) as "identical" and *shakulah* as "broken." He offers two possible meanings for *mat-imot*, either "twins" or "producing twins."

ד:ג כְּחוּט הַשָּׁנִי שִׂפְתוֹתַיִךְ וּמִדְבָּרֵיךְ נָאוֶה כְּפֶלַח הָרִמּוֹן רַקָּתֵךְ מִבַּעַד לְצַמָּתֵךְ:

4:3 YOUR LIPS ARE LIKE A CRIMSON THREAD, AND YOUR MOUTH IS BEAUTIFUL. YOUR FOREHEAD ABOVE YOUR VEIL IS LIKE A SLICE OF POMEGRANATE.

The last clause is difficult to translate. *Rakateich* (your forehead) can also mean "temple," as in the usage of *b'rakato* to refer to Sisera's temple, through which Jael

46

thrust a tent peg (Judges 4:21). In Sisera's case, we imagine that he was sleeping on his side, leaving his temple exposed. In this verse, however, we imagine that the lover is looking straight at his beloved's face. Hence, "forehead" or "brow" would make more sense. As Koehler-Baumgartner (p. 141) points out, *miba-ad* means "from behind." If the beloved's face is hidden by a veil "from behind," then how can the lover see it? Moreover, the image of a "slice of pomegranate" suggests a difference in color between the inside of the fruit and its rind, something light and dark. As a result, we have chosen to translate the last clause as "your forehead above your veil is like a slice of pomegranate."

The *Targum* connects the verse to the High Priest on Yom Kippur, who is able, through his prayer, to atone for the sins of Israel, which resemble a "thread of crimson" (see Isaiah 1:18), and make them white as wool. The "pomegranate" refers to the people's king, who is as full of mitzvot as the fruit is full of seeds. Even the king's advisors are virtuous. Rashi sees the "crimson thread" as a reference to Rahab, who was promised protection from an oncoming attack because she hid the spies; she hung a cord of crimson out of her window to mark it as a place of refuge (Joshua 2:18ff.). On the basis of Ezekiel 33:30 and Malachi 3:16, Rashi reads *midbareich* (your mouth) as "your speech." To make his point, he gives the Old French *parlerin* (Modern French, *parler*), "to speak."

ד:ד כְּמִגְדַּל דָּוִיד צַוָּארֵךְ בָּנוּי לְתַלְפִּיּוֹת אֶלֶף הַמָּגֵן תָּלוּי עָלָיו כֹּל שִׁלְטֵי הַגִּבּוֹרִים:

4:4 YOUR NECK IS LIKE THE TOWER OF DAVID, BUILT FOR [DISPLAYING] WEAPONS. A THOUSAND SHIELDS HANG ON IT, ALL THE QUIVERS OF WARRIORS.

It seems strange to compare a lover's neck to masonry and brick even if the intention is to emphasize strength. The meaning of *talpiyot*, which occurs in the Bible only here, is not clear. Koehler-Baumgartner (p. 1741) joins the word with *banui*, the word that precedes it, to mean "constructed in layers." However, it is difficult to see how "constructed in layers" might be a description of beauty or a compliment. *Banui* generally means "built for," which would bring us back to the question of what *talpiyot* means. Rashi takes the word to mean "beauty" and the phrase *banui l'talpiyot* to mean "built for beauty." He relates the word *talpiyot* to the word *malfeinu* in the phrase *malfeinu mibahamot aretz* (Job 35:11): "He teaches us more wisdom than the animals of the land." His use of *malfeinu* to understand *talpiyot* is not all that helpful, however, since the word *malfeinu* is equally problematic to translate. Not only does it lack a root letter, but the generally accepted meaning is not related to beauty. Elsewhere Rashi translates *malfeinu* as "to teach," as in the phrase from Job. While Ibn Ezra quotes "those who say" that *talpiyot* is related to *malfeinu* he curtly adds "that according to grammarians, *ein lo domeh* [there is no comparison]." Instead, he relates *talpiyot* to two words: *talot piyot* ("hanging of swords," since *peh* can refer to the edge of a sword, as in Genesis 34:26). Perhaps Ibn

Ezra was thinking of the passage in Ezekiel (27:10–11) that describes various pieces of armor hanging on a tower. By combining Rashi and Ibn Ezra's insights into the phrase *banui l'talpiyot,* it is possible to conclude that the author intended to suggest a parallel between a tower as a fitting place to hang weapons as ornaments, and a young woman's neck as a place for the hanging of jewelry as ornaments.

The *Targum* offers a more figurative meaning for the verse. This source reads the verse as a reference to the head of the study academy, whose virtues and good deeds make him akin to King David. By the word of his mouth, the world is built. Through his teaching of Torah, the people of Israel are cleansed and thus will be victorious in each of their battles.

Rashi contends that "shields" implies that the Torah will be Israel's protection; "quivers" are filled with arrows—students of Torah. For Rashi, the "shields" and "quivers" together suggest the hewn stone chamber in the Temple. Ibn Ezra takes the "neck" as a reference to the king and "shields" to refer to the princes.

ד:ה שְׁנֵי שָׁדַיִךְ כִּשְׁנֵי עֳפָרִים תְּאוֹמֵי צְבִיָּה הָרוֹעִים בַּשּׁוֹשַׁנִּים:

4:5 YOUR TWO BREASTS ARE LIKE TWO FAWNS, TWINS OF A
   GAZELLE, FEEDING AMONG THE LILIES.

The *Targum* avoids the literalism of the verse and suggests that the "two breasts" refer to two different Messiahs: one is from the Davidic line *(Mashiach ben David)*; the other is from the line of Ephraim *(Mashiach ben Ephrayim)*. Both resemble Moses and Aaron, who were compared to two young gazelles. Through their merit, the Israelites were provided with sustenance in the wilderness for forty years: they were given manna and quail and the water of Miriam's Well. In a similar fashion, Rashi understands the "two breasts" as standing for Moses and Aaron. Since gazelles often bear "twins," the author implies that Moses and Aaron were equally worthy. As an alternative explanation, Rashi also suggests that the "two breasts" stand for the two tablets of the covenant, with five words set opposite five words. In other words, "I am the Lord" is set against "Don't murder," because murder diminishes God's image. "You shall have no other gods" is set against "Don't commit adultery," because worshiping other gods is like a spouse who betrays a partner by committing adultery. Ibn Ezra views the "two breasts" as the Written Torah and the Oral Torah.

As noted in 2:1, it is difficult to determine the precise identification of the flower *shoshanim.* We again translate it as "lilies."

ד:ו עַד שֶׁיָּפוּחַ הַיּוֹם וְנָסוּ הַצְּלָלִים אֵלֶךְ לִי אֶל־הַר הַמּוֹר וְאֶל־גִּבְעַת הַלְּבוֹנָה:

4:6 WHEN THE BREEZE WILL COOL THE DAY AND THE
SHADOWS WILL FLEE, THEN WILL I GO TO THE MOUNTAIN
OF MYRRH AND THE HILL OF FRANKINCENSE.

Those who have spent time in the desert can understand the feeling created by the speaker. In the heat of the sun, one waits with anticipation for the cooling off that takes place beginning in the late afternoon. Koehler-Baumgartner (p. 917) points out that the phrase *yafuach hayom* (literally, "the day will breathe") refers to "the arrival of the cooling wind in the afternoon."

The last half of the verse may be read as a euphemism for sexual activity rather than as a description of mountain climbing. The *Targum*, however, avoids reading the verse as a poetic description of erotic thoughts. Rather, it suggests that while the Israelites maintained their ancestral connection to God, they were able to fend off all kinds of demons. Because the Divine Presence resided in the Temple on Mount Moriah (the mountain of myrrh), the demons were driven off by the aroma of the incense. For Rashi, the verse evokes the time of loss of divine favor, beginning with and continuing to the time of the two sons of Eli, Hophni and Phinehas (I Samuel 1:3, 4:4). Ibn Ezra understands *ad sheyafuach hayom* as "until the day breathes" and takes the phrase to refer to the spiritual status of the Jewish people. When they follow the mitzvot, the Divine Presence abides among them.

ד:ז כֻּלָּךְ יָפָה רַעְיָתִי וּמוּם אֵין בָּךְ:

4:7 DARLING, YOU ARE ALTOGETHER BEAUTIFUL, THERE IS
NOT A BLEMISH ON YOU.

Here too the *Targum* avoids the simple eroticism of the verse. While this seems to be a statement made by someone looking at or thinking about his lover's naked body, the *Targum* instead understands the verse to reflect God's pleasure with Israel. While the people of Israel follow the will of God, God praises them in heaven and says, "O congregation of Israel, you are altogether beautiful, without a blemish on you." Since Rashi takes the "mountain of myrrh" in 4:6 as a reference to Mount Moriah, he suggests here that when the people of Israel offer sacrifices on that mountain, then they are "altogether beautiful and without blemish." Hence, God will accept their sacrifices.

Ibn Ezra bridges a literal understanding of the verse with a figurative one. He believes that the verse is as if the young woman said: "All that you have is acceptable [literally, 'fine in my eyes']."

אִתִּי מִלְּבָנוֹן כַּלָּה אִתִּי מִלְּבָנוֹן תָּבוֹאִי תָּשׁוּרִי מֵרֹאשׁ אֲמָנָה ד:ח
מֵרֹאשׁ שְׂנִיר וְחֶרְמוֹן מִמְּעֹנוֹת אֲרָיוֹת מֵהַרְרֵי נְמֵרִים:

4:8 O BRIDE, COME FROM LEBANON, COME WITH ME.
COME DOWN FROM THE TOP OF AMANAH, FROM THE
TOP OF SENIR AND HERMON, FROM THE LAIRS OF
LIONS AND THE MOUNTAINS OF LEOPARDS.

We encounter a problem with translation at the very beginning of the verse. If *iti* is
understood simply as a preposition with a first person ending (with me), then the first
three words, the first half of the clause, has no verb. We have adopted the reading of
a number of versions (*Biblia Hebraica*, p. 1205) that translate *iti* as the verb "come,"
from the root *alef-tav-hei*. *Tashuri* comes from *shin-vav-reish*, which, according to
Koehler-Baumgartner (pp. 1450–51), has two different meanings: "gaze," as in
Numbers 23:9, or "bend down," as in Isaiah 57:9. *Biblia Hebraica* (p. 1205) proposes
the emendation of the word to *tasuri* (turn away). Thus, it is a puzzle as to whether to
translate this word as "look down," "bend down," "go down," or "turn away." The
context seems to argue against "gaze" or "look down." The young woman has been
asked twice to come (away), whether *iti* is read as "come" or as "with me,"
emending it to read *tavo-i iti*, "come with me." The young woman is asked to move,
not to look. As difficult as it is to understand some of the descriptions of the woman's
beauty, it is similarly hard to know much about the exact descriptions of the
mountains that are mentioned. Perhaps their highest elevations are moundlike or have
sharp apexes. Hence, we have translated *meirosh* simply as "from the top."

The *Targum* takes *iti* as "with me" in its interpretation of the verse as God's
statement that Israel is like a bride *(ninfei)* being asked to enter with God into the
Temple. (Note that *ninfei*—the word that symbolizes the Jewish people—is from the
Greek loan word *nunpheh*.) The heads of the people who dwell near the Amanah
River and who dwell near a snow-covered mountain bring offerings to the Temple.
The people who are in Hermon offer taxes for those who dwell in the great cities.
Such people are as mighty as lions, for they bring their offerings from the cities of the
mountains that they took over from leopards.

Rashi interprets *iti* as God's statement that when the Jewish people went into exile,
God went with them. When they return from exile, God will return with them. Rashi
takes the word *tashuri* as "you will gaze." Thus, when God will bring together those
who have been exiled, the people will gaze and reflect on the reward for their labors
and their *emunah*, "faithfulness." This is a wordplay on *Amanah*, the place name
mentioned in the verse.

Interpreting the verse literally, Ibn Ezra relates *tashuri* to *ashurenu v'lo karov*, "what
I behold will not come soon" (Numbers 24:17). Hence, he understands the word as
"you will gaze." In his figurative interpretation, Ibn Ezra suggests that "come from
Lebanon" refers to the people of Israel who came from Lebanon to celebrate the
Festivals in Jerusalem. The "lions" and the "leopards" refer to the Babylonians, who
preyed on the people of Israel.

ד:ט לִבַּבְתִּנִי אֲחֹתִי כַלָּה לִבַּבְתִּינִי בְּאַחַת מֵעֵינַיִךְ בְּאַחַד עֲנָק מִצַּוְּרֹנָיִךְ:

4:9 MY SISTER, MY BRIDE, YOU HAVE CAPTIVATED MY HEART WITH ONLY ONE GLANCE, WITH ONLY ONE LINK OF YOUR NECKLACE.

The term "my sister, my bride" may seem like a strange idiom, but most cultures and languages have their own approaches to terms of endearment.

The *Targum* takes the verse as God's statement to the people of Israel, who, like the bride *ninfei*, are sealed upon the divine heart. In this reading, the "glance" (literally, "eye") refers to any of the heads of the Sanhedrin. The "link of...[the] necklace" refers to any of the kings of Judah who would place the royal wreaths on their throats. Rashi explains *libavtini* (you have captivated my heart) as "you have attracted my heart to you." He explains *anak*, "link," first literally and then figuratively, as a reference to the mitzvot that Israel has performed and that join the Jewish people together. As a second figurative interpretation of "link," Rashi suggests that it is a reference to Abraham (based on a reading of Joshua 14:15). According to the Talmud, the giant mentioned in Joshua 14:15 is Abraham (Jerusalem Talmud, *Shabbat* 16:1). Ibn Ezra takes *anak* as a reference to the tribe of Judah, whose piety became the common link among the kings. Ibn Ezra reads "one glance" (literally "one eye") as a reference to Elijah the Prophet, who had moved Israel to repentance.

ד:י מַה-יָּפוּ דֹדַיִךְ אֲחֹתִי כַלָּה מַה-טֹּבוּ דֹדַיִךְ מִיַּיִן וְרֵיחַ שְׁמָנַיִךְ מִכָּל-בְּשָׂמִים:

4:10 HOW DELIGHTFUL ARE YOUR CARESSES, MY SISTER, MY BRIDE. THEY ARE BETTER THAN WINE AND THE AROMA OF YOUR PERFUMES [ARE BETTER] THAN OTHER SPICES.

All of the images presented in this verse have been discussed previously. The idea that "caresses" can intoxicate lovers and that this is better than wine was introduced in 1:4. The role of perfume in lovemaking was introduced in 1:13.

The *Targum* sees in this verse a continuation of the divine love song to God's covenantal partner, the people of Israel. In this reading, the verse comes to mean that Israel is more beloved than all of the seventy nations. Additionally, it suggests that the good name of Israel's righteous people has achieved fame more widespread than the aroma of all spices. Rashi also takes "aroma" as a reference to the good name of the righteous of Israel. He takes the first clause to mean that wherever the Jewish people have worshiped and expressed their love for God, the Divine Presence has rested there. The repentance initiated by Elijah the Prophet, noted by Ibn Ezra in the previous verse, explains his understanding of the first clause of this verse: the "caresses" are Israel's acts of penitence. Gersonides, however, understands the verse to mean that no bodily delights, like that of wine, can match the delight of intellectual achievement.

ד:יא נֹפֶת תִּטֹּפְנָה שִׂפְתוֹתַיִךְ כַּלָּה דְּבַשׁ וְחָלָב תַּחַת לְשׁוֹנֵךְ וְרֵיחַ
שַׂלְמֹתַיִךְ כְּרֵיחַ לְבָנוֹן:

4:11 O BRIDE, YOUR LIPS DRIP WITH PURE HONEY. HONEY
AND MILK ARE BENEATH YOUR TONGUE. THE AROMA
OF YOUR GARMENTS IS LIKE THE AROMA OF LEBANON.

Nofet and *d'vash* refer to two different kinds of honey. Koehler-Baumgartner suggests
that the first is the kind extracted from the honeycomb (p. 714), while the second
term refers to a kind of honey that has been boiled (p. 213). However, the use of
d'vash in Judges 14:8 suggests that the term was probably used to refer to both kinds
of honey. The author was probably employing both terms for artistic purposes.

The *Targum* understands the verse as a reference to the prayers of the priests in the
Temple; their songs of praise are as sweet as honey and milk, and their garments have
the aroma of incense. (The *Targum* employs a wordplay on *ulbanin*, "incense," and
l'vanon, "Lebanon.") Rashi connects the "lips [that] drip with pure honey" to the
ta-amei Torah, "punctuation marks of the Torah" or "the meanings of the Torah."
Likewise, "the aroma of your garments" alludes to the mitzvot related to dress: the
tzitzit (fringes), the blue color *(t'cheilet)* for the *tzitzit*, the garments of the priests, and
the prohibition concerning the mingling of materials *(sha-atneiz)*.

ד:יב גַּן נָעוּל אֲחֹתִי כַלָּה גַּל נָעוּל מַעְיָן חָתוּם:

4:12 MY SISTER, MY BRIDE, YOU ARE A LOCKED-UP GARDEN,
A SPRING THAT HAS STOPPED, A FOUNTAIN THAT IS
SEALED.

While it is impossible to know the author's intention in using the metaphor "a locked-
up garden," the Rabbis understood it as a euphemism for chastity (Babylonian
Talmud, *Yoma* 75a). Perhaps the lover is praising his beloved's chastity and also
rejoicing that she has sexually offered herself to him.

Since the *Targum* consistently reads the Song of Songs as a metaphor of a love song
by God to the people Israel, it understands this verse as a praise of women in general.
The married women of Israel are as modest as brides. Compared to a garden, they are
reminiscent of the Garden of Eden, into which only the souls of the righteous may
enter. The image of a spring in this verse brings to mind the spring of fresh water that
proceeded from the Garden and was the source of the four major ancient rivers. Had
that "spring" not been sealed by God, its waters would have inundated the world.
Rashi also takes the "locked-up garden" as a reference to the modesty of Jewish
women. He offers two meanings for the "stopped spring." The first is a sealed
fountain; the second is a closed gate. Ibn Ezra explains that aromas may escape from
a "locked-up garden," but none may enter it. Hence comes the praise of the lover's
chastity.

If we read this verse as a commentary upon our spiritual quest, we can acknowledge that when God seems difficult to reach, we assume that it is God who is removed and distant, closed, "locked up." Yet, we know it is often we who shut ourselves off from the Divine.

ד:יג שְׁלָחַיִךְ פַּרְדֵּס רִמּוֹנִים עִם פְּרִי מְגָדִים כְּפָרִים עִם־נְרָדִים:

4:13 YOUR SHOOTS ARE A GARDEN OF POMEGRANATES, WITH DELICIOUS FRUITS, WITH HENNA AND NARD.

Although this verse seems straightforward, it contains a variety of challenges. The word *sh'lachayich* occurs only here in the Bible. Our translation of it as "your shoots" follows Koehler-Baumgartner (p. 1517). *Pardeis* (garden) is a Persian loanword that is the basis of the word "paradise." Hence, the word suggests more than a mere "garden." It implies a garden that has been cultivated with great care and expense. Our translation of *p'ri m'gadim* as "delicious fruits" also follows Koehler-Baumgartner (p. 543).

The *Targum* suggests that "shoots" is a reference to the young Jewish men who fulfill the mitzvot and love their spouses and children. Thus, they may be compared to the aromas of the spices in the Garden of Eden. Rashi takes *sh'lachayich* as a reference to a dry land that needs to be irrigated continually so that it can become a "garden of pomegranates." Thus, he sees a similarity between the work of irrigation and the effect of performing mitzvot on the Jewish people. The former causes the fruit to grow and prosper, while the latter does the same for the Jewish people. Ibn Ezra explains that in Arabic, *pardeis* refers to a garden in which only one species grows. Gersonides takes the verse to refer to universal ideas that provide pleasure to the human intellect.

ד:יד נֵרְדְּ וְכַרְכֹּם קָנֶה וְקִנָּמוֹן עִם כָּל־עֲצֵי לְבוֹנָה מֹר וַאֲהָלוֹת עִם כָּל־רָאשֵׁי בְשָׂמִים:

4:14 NARD AND SAFFRON, SPICE REED AND CINNAMON, WITH ALL KINDS OF TREES OF FRANKINCENSE, MYRRH AND ALOES AND WITH THE BEST OF ALL SPICES.

It is difficult to know precisely what is meant by *kaneh* (literally, "reed"). We have followed Koehler-Baumgartner (p. 1113) and translated it as "spice reed." If the image presented is that of a garden, then *atzei l'vonah* would refer to "trees of frankincense." If the author intended to refer to various kinds of aromatic items, then *atzei l'vonah* might be translated as "wood of frankincense."

Perhaps overwhelmed by the repetition of the spices, the *Targum* simply translates the verse literally, word for word. Neither Rashi nor Gersonides chose to comment on the verse. Ibn Ezra's only comment is that *ahalot* (aloes) is also a kind of spice.

ד:טו מַעְיַן גַּנִּים בְּאֵר מַיִם חַיִּים וְנֹזְלִים מִן־לְבָנוֹן:

4:15 A GARDEN SPRING, A WELL OF FRESH WATER, STREAMS
FLOWING DOWN FROM LEBANON.

With this verse, the poet seems to have changed his setting and imagery. But the
impression remains that the author is painting a picture in words of natural beauty.
Here the beloved is no longer compared to a delightful pleasure garden. Now she is
compared to the water that makes life in the garden possible and causes the plants in
it to grow.

The *Targum* reads the verse as a reference to the waters of the pool of Shiloah, as
well as a reference to those waters that flow down from Lebanon and provide water
for the entire Land of Israel. This water results from the virtue of those who study the
words of Torah, often imagined metaphorically as a well of living water. The water is
also connected to the water poured on the altar in the Temple in Jerusalem—which
is also called Lebanon. Rashi explains that this is the water that irrigates the "shoots"
in 4:13. In a second interpretation, he sees this water as a reference to the ritual
immersions of Jewish women (following their menstrual periods).

ד:טז עוּרִי צָפוֹן וּבוֹאִי תֵימָן הָפִיחִי גַנִּי יִזְּלוּ בְשָׂמָיו יָבֹא דוֹדִי לְגַנּוֹ
וְיֹאכַל פְּרִי מְגָדָיו:

4:16 NORTH WIND AWAKE! SOUTH WIND COME! BLOW
UPON MY GARDEN. LET THE AROMA OF ITS SPICES
SPREAD. LET MY LOVER COME TO HIS GARDEN AND EAT
ITS DELICIOUS FRUITS!

The erotic symbolism of this verse is clear, as is its physicality. The garden seems to be
the body of the beloved young woman. In this verse, she invites her lover to enjoy her
garden by making love to her.

The *Targum* reads the verse as a description of the Temple. Thus, "north" refers to
the north side of the Temple, where the table that held the twelve loaves of
showbread was placed. "South" refers to the south side of the Temple, where a lamp
for illumination was located. The priests offered sacrifices on the altar and burned
spices there, as well. The Israelites would say, "Let God, my lover, enter the Temple
and receive with favor the sacrifices of the people."

Rashi understands the verse literally, as the lover's statement to his beloved. Her
fragrance is so pleasing to him that he would command the winds to carry that
fragrance a great distance. Rashi then tells the reader about the various Diaspora
settlements that sent offerings to the Temple and gathered in Jerusalem on the
Festivals. Their presence indicated their expressed hope that God would be present.
Ibn Ezra understands the "north wind" as the wind that blows "when the day
breathes" (see 4:6) and that scatters the spices of the garden.

54

Bat Kol *(Heavenly Voice)*

The *bat kol* is the heavenly or divine voice that reveals the will of God to humankind. According to the Rabbis, the *bat kol* (literally, "daughter of the voice," or a feminine sound of some sort) was already heard in the biblical period (Babylonian Talmud, *Makot* 23b). The talmudic passage refers to the classic story of Solomon's wisdom and the dispute of two women who claim to be the mother of a particular child (see I Kings 3:27); the outcome was determined by a *bat kol*.

When the period of prophecy ended, the *bat kol* served as a means of communication between God and human beings. Usually, the *bat kol* was considered an external voice, but the Rabbis report that it was sometimes heard in dreams (Babylonian Talmud, *Chagigah* 14b). It is cited in two places in the Talmud. In *Eiruvin* 13b, the *bat kol* settles a dispute as to whether the halachah is interpreted correctly by Beit (the House of) Shammai or by Beit Hillel. In *Bava M'tzia* 59b, there is a dispute about whether a certain kind of oven can be considered clean or unclean. However, the authority of the *bat kol* was rejected by Rabbi Y'hoshua, who claimed that Torah is not in heaven and that therefore disputes cannot be resolved in this way. Later, the Rabbis accepted Rabbi Y'hoshua's view (*Bava M'tzia* 59b) and allowed the *bat kol* to function only in controversies between Beit Hillel and Beit Shammai (*Eiruvin* 13b).

Sanhedrin

While the apparent form of the Sanhedrin may have changed over the course of its existence, it was primarily a legislative body that dealt with religious matters. On rare occasions, it acted as a court. It probably existed in the Land of Israel during the Roman period—before and after the destruction of the Temple—until approximately 425 C.E. Hellenistic sources describe the Sanhedrin as a political body of seventy-one judges, led by the High Priest. Rabbinic sources describe it as composed of scholars, led by the *nasi* and the *av beit din*, the leaders of the Pharisees.

The Confrontation of Jacob with Laban (Genesis 29–31)

Laban, Rebekah's brother, was Isaac's brother-in-law. He was also the father of Leah and Rachel, who became Jacob's wives. Though Laban offered Jacob refuge when he fled from his brother Esau, he later deceived Jacob, and their relationship was one of conflict. When Jacob sought to marry Rachel—having paid a "bride's price" of seven years of labor—Laban substituted her sister Leah instead. Jacob was allowed to marry Rachel as well, but only at the price of working another seven years for Laban. Laban also deceived Jacob over his wages. Jacob worked in exchange for what Laban thought were inferior lambs, although they turned out to be the best ones and brought Jacob wealth. Because of the strain in the relationship between the two, Jacob took his family out of Haran, where Laban lived, but Laban pursued them. Eventually, the two antagonists reconciled.

Heave Offerings

"Heave offerings" is the phrase generally used to translate *t'rumah*, "an offering"—which includes all forms of offerings made by the Israelites. The translation intimates the ritual elevation of the offering; the offering was presented to the priest with an up and down motion, which is distinguished from a wave offering (presented with a motion from side to side). The heave offering was the "sacrifice" presented to the priest for his own use.

Hewn Stone Chamber in the Temple

The hewn stone chamber in the Temple was the equivalent of the Supreme Court Building. The Great Sanhedrin, the highest Jewish court, consisted of seventy-one judges. It met in the chamber of hewn stone located on the Temple Mount in Jerusalem. Half of the chamber was situated within the courtyard wall on consecrated ground, while the other half was built outside the courtyard wall on unconsecrated ground. The judges met in the unconsecrated section, since only those descended from the House of David were permitted to sit in the consecrated section. The consecrated area was also used as a chapel for the priests.

The authority of the Sanhedrin was related to where it functioned. If it did not meet in the chamber, the criminal justice system—the court that meted out the death penalty—was prohibited from functioning. According to the Talmud (*Avodah Zarah* 8b), the Sanhedrin left the chamber forty years before the destruction of the Temple. Apparently, the judges did not want the court to be used as an instrument for capital punishment within the context of the Roman occupation.

Mashiach ben Efrayim

Shortly after Solomon's death, the ten northern tribes broke away from the united monarchy, splintering the country into a Northern Kingdom and a Southern Kingdom. Solomon's son Rehoboam, representing the House of David, continued to rule Judah, the Southern Kingdom, while the Northern Kingdom was ruled by Jeroboam son of Nebat, who hailed from the tribe of Ephraim (one of the two tribes that emerged from the line of Joseph). As a result, the Northern Kingdom is often referred to as Ephraim. Thus, Jewish tradition posited two messianic lines. However, according to the Malbim's commentary on the prophecy of Ezekiel 37:21–24, there will be two phases in the redemption of the Jewish people. The *Mashiach ben Efrayim* will be a warrior who will effect the national unification, as prophesied by Ezekiel, before the advent of *Mashiach ben David*. This national unification will be followed by a period of purification and repentance that will usher in the final redemption. The model for this redemption has its roots in the reunification of Joseph with his brothers (Genesis 45:3–4). It also teaches that unity, national renewal, and repentance have intrinsic values that occur in sequence as preludes to complete redemption.

Twelve Loaves of Showbread

The concept of showbread comes from Exodus 25:30, "And you shall set upon the table showbread before Me always," and Leviticus 24:5–9, "You shall take choice flour and bake twelve loaves of it; two-tenths of an ephah shall be in each loaf. You shall place them in two rows, six in a row, on the table of pure gold. You shall put pure frankincense with each row, to be a token offering for the bread, as an offering by fire to *Adonai*. Every Sabbath day Aaron shall set them in order before *Adonai* continuously as a commitment of the people of Israel, as a covenant forever. They shall be for Aaron and his descendants, who shall eat of them in a holy place, for they are most holy portions for him from the offerings by fire to *Adonai*, a perpetual due."

The Hebrew expression *lechem hapanim* literally means "bread of the faces." Rabbi Abraham Mordecai of Gur taught that its appearance was different to each individual, as the person's own nature was reflected in what he or she saw. People with a strong faith in God saw the bread as steaming hot, even days after it had been taken from the oven. Conversely, people of little faith saw the bread as cold and stale, reflecting their own coldness and indifference to the Jewish faith. In explaining the showbread, *Sefer HaChinuch* notes that if ones serves God with physical substance, then one will be blessed with physical prosperity. By bringing the bread to the Tabernacle on a weekly basis, the Jewish people merited physical support.

GLEANINGS

The Attraction of Love to Religion

What makes love so attractive in religion is that "Love upsets the natural order" (Gen. R. 55.8). Its very extremism helps us break through the fascination of everyday profaneness. Consider the rabbis' interpretations of the tripartite behest to love God. "Simeon b. Azzai said: 'with all thy soul,' love God until your soul departs from you" (Ber. 61b). "R. Eliezer said: Since 'with all thy soul' is stated, why is 'with all thy might' stated? Or if 'with all thy might' is desired, why also write 'with all thy soul'? For the one to whom life is more precious than wealth, 'with all thy soul' is written, while he to whom wealth is more precious than life must accept, 'with all thy might'" (San. 74a). Loving God must be paramount. Any lesser love needs to be our instrument in serving God.

And this is exactly our Jewish religious ideal—to learn to love God with an all-powerful, all-consuming passion. The thirteenth-century Franco-German sage Judah the Pious says: "You need to love the Creator with a great and mighty love that makes you lovesick as over a woman, thinking about her constantly—sitting or rising, going or coming. Even when he eats or drinks, his love never ceases. More than that should be our love of God, so that we continually think of *Adonai* (Judah Hehasid, *Sefer Hasidim*, 14). Bahya b. Asher, a Spanish commentator who lived half a century or so after Judah, wants even more: "Although the quality of loving God is indeed great, that of desiring God is even greater. In the case of love, one can occasionally forget the object of his love when he is preoccupied with other matters, but this is not so in the case of desire, which is all-consuming. Even when one is asleep, he sees the object of his desire in a dream. The Psalmist compared his longing for God to a person who extends himself so that he is in danger of dying: 'My soul thirsts for You, my body yearns for You, as a parched and thirsty land that has no water' [Ps. 63:2]" (*Kad Hakemah*).

Eugene B. Borowitz and Frances Weinman Schwartz, *The Jewish Moral Virtues*
(Philadelphia: Jewish Publication Society, 1999), 318

Seeking Rebirth and Intimacy

The text [of the Song of Songs] is a powerfully evocative collection of love poetry.

This is the real stuff of human passion; it would surely make a puritan blush.... The text is redolent of the aroma of spring, filled with descriptions of lush gardens and exquisite flowers, playing on the imagery of spring as a time of hope and rebirth.

So, too, Pesach is deeply connected to the imagery of spring. For just as the earth bursts open with new life and new possibilities in the spring, Pesach celebrates our birth as a people. Just as the flowers emerge in their full beauty after the darkness of winter, our people emerged from slavery into freedom and possibility.

The song dovetails with Pesach in another way, as Pesach is the time that our people's passionate love affair with God began. We did not commit ourselves to God until the giving of the Torah (Shavuot), but the Exodus and the time in the desert—at least as the prophets nostalgically remember it—was the time of passionate love and devotion between Israel and her Beloved.

Reading the Song of Songs, then, is like singing the love songs from the time when our love was young and strong.... We recall the times of great love and intimacy between our people and God....

Amy Eilberg, "Hol Hamo'ed Pesach: Seeking Rebirth, Intimacy,"
Torah Thoughts, *Jewish Bulletin of Northern California*, April 2, 1999

Ritually Transporting

Judaism suggests that the profundity and purity of human commitment implied by a wedding make it possible to believe in a fully transformed, healed world. The bride and groom, the *Sheva Berakhot* seem to imply, are not simply the two people of flesh and blood getting married. They are the perfected, idealized loving companions, Adam and Eve in the Garden of Eden. The purity of their love rekindles our dream of a wholly pure existence, the Garden of Eden. Jewish tradition asserts that their commitment to each other furthers God's process of creation, bringing the world one step closer to its eventual perfection. The bride and groom are also the young men and women of a rebuilt Jerusalem, whose love bespeaks perfection, salvation, redemption of the Jewish people, and, ultimately, the world.

Though when we are at a wedding we are often focused on the people involved and the moment at hand, the richness of this Jewish ritual—symbolism combined with liturgy—seeks to transport us, even momentarily, to a very different time and place. If we allow it to, the wedding—like Shabbat—transforms us and places us in a transformed world, challenging us, in turn, to use our energies to create it.

Daniel Gordis, *God Was Not in the Fire: The Search for a Spiritual Judaism*
(New York: Scribner, 1993), 123–24

Divine Loving

In our hearts we crave to hear one message—are we loved? Times occur when we know that there are no accidents in the world. God is a loving that is vaster than a parent's loving. This caring One who holds us in pleasure and in pain, who wills us to grow toward Her/Him-self. This is God, the *Ahavah Rabbah*, the great love.

That two bodies attract each other in space, the law of gravity is God, the loving, the flow in which people care for each other, the flow in which a cat licks her kittens clean, the flow in which if you ask a question "Why?" and there is another person caring enough to respond and to provide an answer. And the "Because" that makes sense because answering is a basic form of caring, which coming from God we call revelation. And when we pray and we feel we are attended to, that loving is God. So too is the wanting to make babies, and willingness to labor in giving birth, and the nursing that comes close to the heart, that is the loving godding. The arms that wait to receive one old and worn, one fatally injured and dying, that too is that divine loving.

Zalman Schachter-Shalomi, in *Paradigm Shift:*
From the Jewish Renewal Teachings of Reb Zalman Schachter-Shalomi,
ed. Ellen Singer (Northvale, NJ: Jason Aronson, 1993), 136

CHAPTER FIVE

ה:א בָּאתִי לְגַנִּי אֲחֹתִי כַלָּה אָרִיתִי מוֹרִי עִם־בְּשָׂמִי אָכַלְתִּי יַעְרִי
עִם־דִּבְשִׁי שָׁתִיתִי יֵינִי עִם־חֲלָבִי אִכְלוּ רֵעִים שְׁתוּ וְשִׁכְרוּ דּוֹדִים:

5:1 I HAVE COME INTO MY GARDEN, MY SISTER, MY BRIDE.
I HAVE GATHERED MY MYRRH AND MY SPICES, I HAVE
EATEN MY HONEYCOMB WITH MY HONEY, I HAVE
DRUNK MY WINE AND MY MILK. EAT FRIENDS, EAT AND
BE DRUNK ON LOVE.

The erotic imagery is clear. The lover has come into his "garden." He has made love
to the one he loves. The *Targum*, rather than reading the verse literally, understands it
as God's response to the Jewish people for having built the Temple, referred to here
metaphorically as the garden. As a reward, God will cause the Divine Presence to rest
therein. Furthermore, God will accept the incense offered by the people. God will
have heavenly fire consume the sacrifices on the altar and, with divine favor, God
will accept the wine offering. God then tells the priests—who love God's instructions
to them—to consume what remains.

Rashi also takes the "garden" as a reference to the Temple, reading the verse as a
whole as a reference to the dedication of the Temple. Rashi understands the first
clause as the divine response to this event, and "myrrh and spices" as the incense
offering at the dedication by the princes. Rashi thinks that the last clause was directed
at the priests of the Temple at that time and to Aaron and his sons at the earlier Tent
of Meeting. In his literal interpretation, Ibn Ezra explains the uncommon word *ariti* as
"gathered." More figuratively, he explains "I have eaten" as the manner in which the
Divine Presence provides for the angels.

ה:ב אֲנִי יְשֵׁנָה וְלִבִּי עֵר קוֹל דּוֹדִי דוֹפֵק פִּתְחִי־לִי אֲחֹתִי רַעְיָתִי יוֹנָתִי
תַמָּתִי שֶׁרֹאשִׁי נִמְלָא־טָל קְוֻצּוֹתַי רְסִיסֵי לָיְלָה:

5:2 I WAS ASLEEP, BUT MY HEART WAS AWAKE. HARK! MY
LOVER KNOCKS. LET ME IN, MY SISTER, MY DARLING,
MY LOVE, MY INNOCENT GIRL. MY HEAD IS WET WITH
DEW, MY CURLS WITH THE SPRAY OF NIGHT.

The young woman recounts her dream that is filled with yearning. Her lover is outside
her room, asking for permission to enter. As in the previous verses, the sexual
symbolism is obvious to the reader. These images also speak to those reading this text

as a metaphor about experiencing a spiritual union with God. For the *Targum*, this verse is a description of the Babylonian exile. The exile was like a nightmare, being asleep and unable to wake up. According to the *Targum*'s way of reshaping the text, God tried to wake the Israelites up with these words: "My beloved Israel, 'Open your mouth and shout, sing My praises, for your tears have touched Me.'" Rashi suggests that "I was asleep" refers to the self-satisfied status of the Jewish people during the period of the First Temple. For him, "my heart was awake" refers to God's ongoing care of the sinning people. "My lover knocks" alludes to the prophets who were dispatched to warn the people, and "let me in" are the words God uses to implore the people to repent. Rashi sees the "dew" and "spray of night" as images derived from the human experience of a lover knocking on the door of his beloved. Ibn Ezra takes "my lover knocks" as a reference to God stirring up the spirit of Cyrus, king of Persia, who eventually ends the exile of the people from the Land in an act of love on God's behalf.

הג פָּשַׁטְתִּי אֶת־כֻּתָּנְתִּי אֵיכָכָה אֶלְבָּשֶׁנָּה רָחַצְתִּי אֶת־רַגְלַי אֵיכָכָה
אֲטַנְּפֵם:

5:3 I HAVE TAKEN OFF MY ROBE. SHALL I PUT IT ON AGAIN? I HAVE WASHED MY FEET. SHALL I DIRTY THEM AGAIN?

The word *eichachah* (how) is found twice in this verse. Since it is a word used to introduce rhetorical questions, we have chosen to not translate it. The verse continues the dream that was recounted in the previous verse.

The first part of the verse is seen by the *Targum* as a confession by the congregation of Israel. The Jewish people had cast off the yoke of the commandments and had followed the abominations of the nations. Following a change of heart, they wanted to repent. The second part of the verse is the divine response to their request, as reported by the prophets. Having removed the Divine Presence from their midst, God will not return it as long as the people continue in their wicked ways. Rashi also takes the verse as the words of errant Israel asking for forgiveness. Having learned the sinful ways from others, the people now fear that they will not be able to return to God, even if they repent. The first clause is read by Ibn Ezra as an indication that those exiled in Babylonia had waited too long before returning to the Land to rebuild the Temple.

הד דּוֹדִי שָׁלַח יָדוֹ מִן־הַחֹר וּמֵעַי הָמוּ עָלָיו:

5:4 MY BELOVED PUT HIS HAND THROUGH THE HOLE,
AND MY ENTIRE BEING WRITHED FOR HIM.

Although the literal meaning of *chor* (hole) is unclear, the author's intent seems obvious. *Chor* may refer to something on the door, perhaps a latch—as in the door to a bedroom. Koehler-Baumgarten (p. 348) suggests that it is a euphemism for sexual entry. On the other hand, *mei-ai*, translated here as "my entire being," literally means "my bowels." This could be translated literally as "my insides writhed for him." If we are willing to emend the text slightly, as Kittel suggests (p. 1206), then *alav* (for him) becomes *alai* (for me, upon me), a reading with which Rashi agrees. Since this is an erotic love poem, it makes more sense to read this verse quite literally: "My lover entered me, and I shook all over with passion for him," a translation attested to by Isaiah 57:8 and Koehler-Baumgarten (p. 387). *Chor* is explained by Rashi as the opening next to the door, while Ibn Ezra reads *chor* as the space between two doors. Ibn Ezra also takes it to mean the window of the heavens through which the divine lover directed the prophets.

The *Targum* uses the verse as an opportunity to teach the reader some highlights of Jewish history. When the Israelites were unwilling to proceed directly to the Land of Israel, God sent the tribes of Reuben, Gad, and Manasseh to cross the Jordan. However, Shalmaneser attacked, defeated them, and carried them off to Halah, Habor, and the area around the Gozan River (II Kings 18:11). (In the account of I Chronicles 5:26, these three tribes are carried away by Pul and Tiglath-pilneser.)

הːה קַמְתִּי אֲנִי לִפְתֹּחַ לְדוֹדִי וְיָדַי נָטְפוּ־מוֹר וְאֶצְבְּעֹתַי מוֹר עֹבֵר עַל
כַּפּוֹת הַמַּנְעוּל:

5:5 I ROSE TO OPEN UP FOR MY LOVER. MY HANDS DRIPPED WITH MYRRH, MY FINGERS WITH DROPS OF MYRRH ON THE HANDLES OF THE LOCK.

The word *oveir* (from *ayin-bet-reish*, "to pass over") is difficult to translate in this context. The phrase *mor oveir* could be translated as "flowing myrrh" or "choice myrrh" (based on *oveir lasocheir*, "acceptable to the merchant" [Genesis 23:16]). We have followed Koehler-Baumgartner (p. 779), which notes the use of the root in Job 6:15 and 11:16 to mean "drain away water." This verse is a continuation of the young woman's dream. The imagery of "opening up" is clearly more than the opening of a door. Perhaps she readied herself for him by lubricating herself either manually or with the use of herbs. Nevertheless, even if the reference is to a part of her body, as it appears to be, it is clear that in doing so, she is opening her entire self to him. Similarly, we must ready ourselves for any relationship, particularly one with the Divine. Some suggest that *shuckling* (the swaying, rocking motion in prayer) helps to do so as we disorient ourselves spatially.

The *Targum* takes the verse to refer to the various offerings brought by the priest who did not gain divine favor because God blocked the gates of repentance. The references to myrrh are seen by Rashi as alluding to Israel's wholehearted compliance with God's requests. Ibn Ezra reads "I rose" as a reference to the building of the Temple and to Israel's hope that the Divine Presence would always abide among them. Gersonides believes that the verse suggests the intellect's preparation for thought.

הֵ:ו פָּתַחְתִּי אֲנִי לְדוֹדִי וְדוֹדִי חָמַק עָבָר נַפְשִׁי יָצְאָה בְדַבְּרוֹ בִּקַּשְׁתִּיהוּ
וְלֹא מְצָאתִיהוּ קְרָאתִיו וְלֹא עָנָנִי:

5:6 I OPENED UP FOR MY LOVER, BUT HE WAS GONE!
I BECAME SO WEAK WHEN HE SPOKE. I LOOKED FOR
HIM, BUT I COULD NOT FIND HIM. I CALLED TO HIM,
BUT HE DID NOT ANSWER.

Translating each clause of this verse idiomatically is difficult. The spiritual seeker who searches for the Divine but cannot find God may be weakened by the fruitless search. We call to God and become frustrated when we hear no answer. The two verbs *chamak avar* (turn and pass away) are used to stress how quickly the lover has vanished; thus, we have rendered it as "he was gone." The use of the verb *yatz'ah* (go out) with the noun *nefesh* (soul) suggests utter weakness, as in the description of the last moments of Rachel's life (Genesis 35:18). Therefore, we have translated *nafshi yatz'ah v'dab'ro* as "I became so weak when he spoke." We take this statement as the young woman's explanation of why she delayed answering the knock of her lover (or his request for her physical love). Idiomatically, the phrase might be translated as "I almost passed out when I heard him speak."

This verse is read by the *Targum* as a response by Israel to God's hiding of divine love. The people say that although they are willing to accept divine instruction, God has removed the Divine Presence from among them. Israel seeks that Presence but cannot find it. Although they pray, God has clouded the heavens, preventing their prayers from reaching the Divine. Rashi explains the verse as a reference to the hiding of the Divine Presence. Because the beloved was not willing to open up for her lover, the lover was not willing to enter. For Ibn Ezra, "when he spoke" is a reference to the past, in 4:1ff., when the two lovers spoke to each other.

הֵ:ז מְצָאֻנִי הַשֹּׁמְרִים הַסֹּבְבִים בָּעִיר הִכּוּנִי פְצָעוּנִי נָשְׂאוּ אֶת־רְדִידִי
מֵעָלַי שֹׁמְרֵי הַחֹמוֹת:

5:7 THE GUARDS WHO PATROL THE CITY FOUND ME. THEY
HIT ME. THEY HURT ME. THOSE WHO GUARD THE
WALLS RIPPED OFF MY MANTLE.

Although we have already met "the (patrolling) guards" in 3:3, their appearance in this verse does not seem to be part of reality. While interpretations of "the guards" vary, including those of a sexual nature, perhaps the guards are simply those people who prevent the lovers from meeting.

The *Targum* connects the verse to the sad events described in II Kings 25:4ff., in which the army of the Chaldeans besieged Jerusalem, conquered it, and captured King Zedekiah. He was stripped of his royal robes, blinded, and taken in chains to Babylonia. Rashi explains that "the guards" are those who arrest the thieves who go about at night. Ibn Ezra takes "the guards" to be the kings of Greece, and the ripping off of "the mantle" to mean the Jewish people who are bereft of the mitzvot.

ה:ח הִשְׁבַּעְתִּי אֶתְכֶם בְּנוֹת יְרוּשָׁלָם אִם־תִּמְצְאוּ אֶת־דּוֹדִי מַה־תַּגִּידוּ
לוֹ שֶׁחוֹלַת אַהֲבָה אָנִי:

5:8 O DAUGHTERS OF JERUSALEM, I ADJURE YOU, THAT IF YOU FIND MY LOVER, DON'T TELL HIM THAT I AM LOVESICK.

The "daughters of Jerusalem" were first encountered in 3:5. In this verse, we follow Koehler-Baumgartner (p. 155) in translating *mah* as a negative participle, "don't." This verse too appears to be part of the young woman's dream. Her pursuit of her lover displays her need for him, but the verbal expression of such a need seems difficult for her. In the same way that we are often without words as we approach the Divine, she doesn't know what to say or how to express what she feels.

The verse is read by the *Targum* as Israel's plea to the prophets, asking them to convey the message of Israel's love to God. The verse is understood by Rashi as a statement of the nations who were astounded by the devotion of Hananiah, Mishael, and Azariah (renamed Shadrach, Meshach, and Abed-nego), Daniel, and Mordecai. The first three were willing to be cast into the fiery furnace rather than worship an idol (Daniel 3:13ff.), Daniel was willing to be cast into a lions' den rather than cease his prayers (Daniel 7:16ff.), and Mordecai was willing to risk his life in the face of Haman's wrath (Esther 3:2ff.). Ibn Ezra understands "I am lovesick" as Israel's statement that in spite of being lax in observance, they retain their love for God; they have not turned to idolatry. For Gersonides, "I am lovesick" suggests the soul's intense yearning to apprehend the truth and its willingness to subordinate all its capacities to the intellect.

ה:ט מַה־דּוֹדֵךְ מִדּוֹד הַיָּפָה בַּנָּשִׁים מַה־דּוֹדֵךְ מִדּוֹד שֶׁכָּכָה הִשְׁבַּעְתָּנוּ:

5:9 O MOST BEAUTIFUL AMONG WOMEN, WHAT IS SPECIAL ABOUT YOUR BELOVED THAT YOU SO ADJURE US?

This statement seems part of the ongoing dream from the previous verses. The "daughters of Jerusalem" ask the young woman about her lover and praise her beauty as well. We have translated *mah dodeich midod* (literally, "what is your beloved more than a beloved?") into idiomatic English as "What is [so] special about your beloved?"

The *Targum* takes the verse as the question put by the prophets to the people of Israel: as the "most beautiful" among the peoples, what deity do you wish to serve? The nations of the world put the same question to Israel in Rashi's interpretation: what is so special about your God that you are willing to suffer martyrdom?

הי דּוֹדִי צַח וְאָדוֹם דָּגוּל מֵרְבָבָה:

5:10 RADIANT AND RUDDY IS MY BELOVED, OUTSTANDING AMONG TEN THOUSAND.

In the dream interpretation, here the "daughters of Jerusalem" receive their answer. The *Targum* takes the verse as the praise given by Israel to God, saying that the God whom we worship is served by hosts (specifically, "ten thousand") of angels. God is garbed by day in a robe as white as snow, and the divine glory is as bright as a flame. Because of God's great wisdom, each day God develops new traditions and will proclaim them to the people. Rashi explains *tzach* (radiant) as "white" and *adom* (ruddy) as a mark of masculine beauty. Ibn Ezra takes *tzach* to reflect Israel's actions, which are pure, and *adom* to reflect the punishment for those who would attack Israel.

ה:יא רֹאשׁוֹ כֶּתֶם פָּז קְוֻצּוֹתָיו תַּלְתַּלִּים שְׁחֹרוֹת כָּעוֹרֵב:

5:11 HIS HEAD IS FINE GOLD. HE HAS CURLY LOCKS, WHICH ARE RAVEN BLACK.

If we did not keep in mind that the young woman is recounting her dream for the reader, and hence her words need not be taken literally, it might be difficult to understand how someone with dark hair in ringlets could be described as having a "head" of "fine gold."

It is the Torah, according to the *Targum*, that is more precious than "fine gold." There are layers of meaning that can be found in its words. Those who keep its words will be as white (i.e., pure) as snow. Those who do not keep them will be as black (guilty) as the wings of a raven. The layers of meaning found in the *Targum* are found as well in the midrash (*Tanchuma, B'reishit* 1:1), which plays on the word *k'vutzotav* (his locks). The midrash argues that in every *kotz* (literally, "thorn," but here used to mean the calligraphic elongation of a letter, called by some "jot and tittle") there is an additional layer of meaning. The significant difference between the Hebrew letter *dalet* and the letter *reish* is the *kotz*, which extends the line of the *reish* to form a *dalet* and adds meaning to the text. There is a difference between the words *echad* (one) and *acheir* (someone else or other)—*echad* ends in *dalet*, while *acheir* ends in *reish*. This difference is particularly important in the *Sh'ma*, the basic statement of Jewish belief, as one letter could change the core theology of the Jewish people. Rashi explains the verse as a metaphor using terms that indicate male beauty. Ibn Ezra's interest in this verse focuses on *paz* (fine gold), which he translates as "precious stones," and *k'vutzotav*, "part of his hair."

ה:יב עֵינָיו כְּיוֹנִים עַל־אֲפִיקֵי מָיִם רֹחֲצוֹת בֶּחָלָב יֹשְׁבוֹת עַל־מִלֵּאת:

5:12 HIS EYES ARE LIKE DOVES NEAR BROOKS. THEY ARE BATHED IN MILK AND WELL SET.

It may be difficult for the modern reader to relate to the images of this verse. How is "doves near brooks" a fitting description of a lover's eyes? Perhaps "bathed in milk" means that his eyes are not reddened by the sun and the dust of the wilderness. In addition, there may be cultural issues or class distinctions implicit in these statements. Even so, they are not familiar, contemporary descriptions of male beauty. Nor would they probably be used to describe God, even in anthropomorphic, gendered terms. These specific physical descriptions may make it difficult to read the text as an allegory, reflecting a relationship between God and the individual, rather than as a simple series of love poems.

The *Targum*, however, consistently reads this text allegorically. Since the *Targum* takes the lover to be God, it is the divine "eyes" that are directed for the benefit and blessing of Jerusalem, as they are turned in that direction. They are also as persistent in their gaze as "doves near brooks." Such divine concern is due to the merit of the judges in the Sanhedrin, who study Torah and clarify the Law so that it can be as smooth as milk. They dwell in study houses and are deliberate in their judgment when dealing with the innocent and the guilty. For Rashi, the entire verse suggests the outstanding beauty of the lover, while Ibn Ezra takes "eyes" to refer to the divine lover and "bathed in milk" to mean that those "eyes" are too pure to gaze at evil.

ה:יג לְחָיָו כַּעֲרוּגַת הַבֹּשֶׂם מִגְדְּלוֹת מֶרְקָחִים שִׂפְתוֹתָיו שׁוֹשַׁנִּים נֹטְפוֹת מוֹר עֹבֵר:

5:13 HIS CHEEKS ARE SPICE BEDS, MOUNDS OF PERFUMES. HIS LIPS ARE LIKE LILIES, DRIPPING MYRRH.

The word *migd'lot* (towers), as it appears in this verse, presents a challenge to translation. Koehler-Baumgartner (p. 544) suggests a change in the vocalization of the word in order to read it as *m'gad'lot* (growing, producing). Such a change would follow the *Targum*, which translates *migd'lot* as *marb'yan* (producing). This vocalization is employed in Psalm 18, which forms part of the Blessing after Meals (*Birkat HaMazon)*. On weekdays, we recite *magdil y'shuot* ("God provides great salvation," from Psalm 18:51); on Sabbaths and Festivals, we recite *migdol y'shu-ot* ("God is a tower of salvation," from II Samuel 22:51, where the Psalm is repeated and the vocalization is changed).

We have followed the translation of both Rashi and Ibn Ezra, who read the word as *migdol* (tower). Whether to read *migd'lot* (towers, mounds) or *m'gad'lot* (growing, producing) depends on how we read the verse. If we want to read it as a description of the contours of the cheek, which is likened to "spice beds," then it is *migd'lot*, "mounds." However, if we see it as parallel to the verb of the second clause *not'fot*

66

(drip), then it is *m'gad'lot* (produce). A similar discussion appears in the commentary to 5:5 regarding *mor oveir* (flowing or choice myrrh). Rashi takes the "mounds of perfumes" to refer to the work of the perfumer. Ibn Ezra reads "his lips" as an allusion to angels, such as Gabriel, who are sent to interact with humans.

The "cheeks" are understood by the *Targum* to refer to the two tablets of the Law given by God to the people. When these tablets are properly understood, they contain so many details that they can be compared to a garden filled with all kinds of spices. The scholars who deal with the Law produce various explanations, and their words are like choice myrrh.

הֶיד יָדָיו גְּלִילֵי זָהָב מְמֻלָּאִים בַּתַּרְשִׁישׁ מֵעָיו עֶשֶׁת שֵׁן מְעֻלֶּפֶת
סַפִּירִים:

5:14 HIS HANDS ARE RODS OF GOLD INSET WITH TOPAZ. HIS BODY IS A PLAQUE OF IVORY DECORATED WITH SAPPHIRES.

We have followed Koehler-Baumgartner in our translation of *tarshish* as "topaz" (p. 1798) and the uncommon word *eshet* as "plaque" (p. 898). The *Targum* sees the verse as a reference to the names of Jacob's sons, the twelve tribes, inscribed on a gold tablet. This is based on the frontlet of gold mentioned in Exodus 28:36. However, no mention is made in that verse of inscribing the tribal names. Those names, according to the *Targum*, were then inscribed on twelve precious stones, together with the names of the Patriarchs (unlike the engraving described in Exodus 28:9–11, which was to be done on two stones with no mention of the Patriarchs). For the names of the precious stones, we have followed those suggested by the new Jewish Publication Society translation (Exodus 28:17–20), on the assumption that they are as accurate as listings in comparable scholarly dictionaries. The name Reuben was to be engraved on carnelian, Simon on chrysolite, Levi on emerald, Judah on turquoise, Issachar on sapphire, Zebulun on amethyst, Dan on jacinth, Naphtali on agate, Gad on crystal, Asher on beryl, Joseph on lapis lazuli, and Benjamin on jasper.

After explaining the literal meaning of the words, Rashi interprets the phrase "doves near brooks" (5:12) as the scholars studying Torah in synagogues and study houses. "Bathed in milk" (5:12) suggests to him their precision in deducing the law. "His cheeks" (5:13) are God's words at Mount Sinai, and "rods of gold" (5:14) are the divine words that bring good to the world. "Inset with topaz" (5:14) indicates the ten words that include the 613 commandments. Ibn Ezra adds that the verse refers to Ezekiel's so-called chariot vision (Ezekiel 1), as explained in the introduction (p. xi), which formed the basis for much of Jewish mysticism. The "rods" are the wheels of the chariot, and the *tarshish* is the precious stone that is mentioned there (Ezekiel 1:15–16).

ה:טו שׁוֹקָיו עַמּוּדֵי שֵׁשׁ מְיֻסָּדִים עַל־אַדְנֵי־פָז מַרְאֵהוּ כַּלְּבָנוֹן בָּחוּר
כָּאֲרָזִים:

5:15 His legs are like pillars of marble set in sockets
of fine gold. His appearance is like the Lebanon,
as remarkable as the cedars.

These images of handsome, strong men are part of the ongoing allegory for the *Targum*, which reads "his legs" as a reference to the righteous whose virtue supports the world. The "fine gold" is the words of Torah that direct the Jewish people to follow the will of God.

Rashi explains that "pillars" refers to the sections of the Torah. "His appearance is like the Lebanon" means that those who study and reflect on those sections will derive great benefit. They will always be able to gain new insights as a result. For Ibn Ezra, "his appearance is like the Lebanon" simply means that the woman's lover is handsome. He also suggests that just as Lebanon contains so many marvelous trees that people think that if they were merely to enter the land, they would find a superb tree, so too it is with God, whose every act is marvelous.

ה:טז חִכּוֹ מַמְתַקִּים וְכֻלּוֹ מַחֲמַדִּים זֶה דוֹדִי וְזֶה רֵעִי בְּנוֹת יְרוּשָׁלָם:

5:16 His mouth is sweet. Everything about him is
delightful. This is my beloved. This is my darling,
O daughters of Jerusalem.

The author shows the readers how much in love the female half of this pair of lovers is. Making reference to the divine lover, the *Targum* explains that the words of God's palate are as sweet as honey; all of the mitzvot are like gold and silver to those who are wise. Such is the praise of God, the friend of Israel, teaches the *Targum*. Beloved are God's prophets who prophesy in Jerusalem. Rashi follows the *Targum* in suggesting that the divine words are sweet, because God can be depended upon to reward the righteous.

Shalmaneser

Shalmaneser (d. ca. 1290 B.C.E.), the son of Hadad-nirari I, succeeded his father as king of Assyria in around the year 1310 B.C.E. During his reign, he carried on a series of campaigns against the Aramaeans in northern Mesopotamia, annexed a portion of Cilicia to the Assyrian empire, and established Assyrian colonies on the borders of Cappadocia. According to his own records which were discovered at Assur, in his first year he conquered eight countries in the north-west and destroyed the fortress of Arinnu, the dust of which he brought to Assur when he restored the temple there. In his second year he defeated Sattuara, king of Malatia, and his Hittite allies, and conquered the whole country as far south as Carchemish. He established a royal residence at Nineveh, and removed the capital from Assur to Calah, approximately 18 miles south of Nineveh.

Pul and Tiglath-pilneser

Tiglath-pilneser, also known as Tiglath-pileser and his Assyrian throne name of Pul, founded what was called the Second Assyrian Empire. He was determined to establish an empire that would encompass the entire world and whose center would be in Nineveh. In the fifth year of his reign (ca. 741 B.C.E.), he appears in Assyrian records as victorious over Azariah (identified as Uzziah in II Chronicles 26:1), king of Judah. However, he is first mentioned in the *Tanach* when he is victorious over Pekah, king of Israel, and Rezin, king of Damascus, who were allies. He put Rezin to death and punished Pekah by taking control of a large part of his kingdom. Tiglath-pilneser also took into captivity a large number of inhabitants from the tribes of Reuben and Gad and as many as half the tribe of Manasseh (II Kings 15:29, 16:5–9; I Chronicles 5:6, 5:26). It was also recorded in Assyrian records that Tiglath-pilneser held court at Damascus and received tribute from neighboring kings, including Pekah of Samaria and Yahu-khazi of Judah, identified as King Ahaz (cf. II Kings 16:10–16).

Hananiah, Mishael, and Azariah

According to the Book of Daniel (chapter 3), Nebuchadnezzar, king of Babylon, erected a statue of gold in the Valley of Dura and decreed that anyone who would not bow down to it would be tossed into a fiery furnace. All the nations of the world agreed to do so except for three young Jews: Hananiah, Mishael, and Azariah (whose names were changed to Shadrach, Meshach, and Abed-nego in Daniel 1:7). The king followed through on his decree and ordered them thrown into the fire. According to the narrative account in Daniel, God sent an angel, who protected them from the flames. When Nebuchadnezzar witnessed the miracles, he released them and praised God as a result.

Divine Glory

It is as difficult to translate the term "divine glory" as it is to explain. The Torah understands "divine glory" as the clouds that hovered over the Israelites during their desert journey. Their presence signified God's presence with the people, as it communicated God's desires to the people, as well: "Whenever a cloud lifted from the Tent [of Meeting], the Israelites would set out accordingly; and at the spot where the cloud settled, there the Israelites would make camp" (Numbers 9:17).

Ten Words

According to the Rabbis of *Pirkei Avot* (5:1), the world was created by means of ten words or utterances. The mystics believe that these words were closely related to the Ten Commandments (also known in Hebrew as "ten utterances").

GLEANINGS

Men Learning from Women

With a woman, a man learns by example what proper desire is. Woman not only begins the partnership of creation, which until now was God's alone, she also offers a new vision of humanness that harkens back to God's original plan. In this homiletic reading of her punishment [to bear children in pain] lies the seed of the redemption of male–female relationships. Let men model themselves after women sexually. Perhaps then we can get back to the first harmony when we were joined as one.

Elyse Goldstein, *ReVisions: Seeing Torah through a Feminist Lens*
(Woodstock, VT: Jewish Lights, 1998), 57

Being a More Loving Person

Love is a feeling. Can we be commanded to feel something? We either feel something or we don't. However, the Torah would not have commanded us to feel something if it were not possible. The Alter Rebbe, Rabbi Schneur Zalman of Lubavitch, responded to this question at length in *Tanya*, his masterpiece. In essence, most of the book is a response to the question of how to love God. The rebbe recommended that we train ourselves to realize that everything we see is the outer garments of God. Everything was created by God. God is within everything and everyone, animating and sustaining all reality. When we penetrate the underlying reality of life, we are naturally filled with love and gratitude for God. He also said that by learning Torah and doing God's Will, a person will be brought to love naturally. The head of a person is located higher than the heart because what we think influences what we feel. By thinking proper thoughts, we arouse the heart to love.

Melinda Ribner, *New Age Judaism: Ancient Wisdom for the Modern World*
(Deerfield Beach, FL: Simcha Press, 2000), 124

The Mission of Israel

There are many Jews in our generation who would be true to the election, covenant, and mission, if these were given a contemporary significance shorn of the supernatural and grounded in historic experience. For such Jews the meaning of Israel lies in our people's millennial quest for the word of God and in the unique way in which this quest unfolded. A passion for justice, freedom, and peace has led the Jewish people to assume an unmistakable identity of its own, regardless of where and when it has lived, what garb it has worn, and what language it has spoken. At one and the same time we Jews have sought to keep alive and enhance this identity and asked others to share our ideals, ideals which have never been limited by either time or geographic boundaries. In our vision [the hu]man is the center of creation, this world is the scene of it, ethical commitment is the heart of it, and a better life for the whole human race is the goal of it.

> Joseph Narot, "The Nature and Destiny of Israel," in *Contemporary Reform Jewish Thought*, ed. Bearnard Martin (Chicago: CCAR and Quadrangle Books, 1968), 142

The Measure of Success

Success has nothing to do with size or numbers, with material possessions or fame. Life is counted in terms of growth and goodness. Someone once said that our purpose in living is not to get ahead of others but to get ahead of ourselves, always to play a better game of life. That's what success is all about. Have we done our best? Are we continuing to grow? Are we more sensitive and compassionate today than we were yesterday? Have we learned to overcome our fears and accept our failures? Do we count our blessings in such a way that we make our blessings count? That's the meaning of success. In the words of Albert Schweitzer: "The great secret of success is to go through life as a person who never gets used up. Grow into your ideals so that life can never rob you of them."

> Sally Preisand, "Address in Honor of the Twentieth Year of Women's Ordination," *Yearbook of the Central Conference of American Rabbis* 101-2 (1993): 183

CHAPTER SIX

וּ:א אָנָה הָלַךְ דּוֹדֵךְ הַיָּפָה בַּנָּשִׁים אָנָה פָּנָה דוֹדֵךְ וּנְבַקְשֶׁנּוּ עִמָּךְ:

6:1 WHERE DID YOUR LOVER GO, O MOST BEAUTIFUL
AMONG WOMEN, TO WHERE HAS HE DISAPPEARED?
LET'S LOOK FOR HIM TOGETHER.

The spiritual journey is not one to be taken alone. Addressing the idea of community, the *Targum* reads the "most beautiful among women" as the congregation of Israel. The "lover" in this verse is God, and those asking the questions are the prophets, who ask, "What did Israel do to cause God to remove the Divine Presence from among the people? Where did God go when God turned away from the Temple?" The people of Israel answer, "Sin and rebellion caused God to leave." The prophets respond, "Then repent, O Israel. Together we will pray and ask for divine mercy." For Rashi, the same questions are posed by the nations who mock Israel, asking, in essence, "Why has God forsaken you?"

וּ:ב דּוֹדִי יָרַד לְגַנּוֹ לַעֲרוּגוֹת הַבֹּשֶׂם לִרְעוֹת בַּגַּנִּים וְלִלְקֹט שׁוֹשַׁנִּים:

6:2 HE HAS GONE DOWN TO THE GARDEN, TO THE SPICE
BED, TO GRAZE IN THE GARDENS AND TO PICK LILIES.

As at the end of chapter 4 and the beginning of chapter 5, the author writes with explicit erotic symbolism. However, it is not clear whether the poet wants to present this verse as a recollection of what happened in a kind of daydream, or as a fantasy of what the young woman would like to happen.

In the interpretation of the *Targum*, this verse represents the divine acceptance of the prayers of the prophets and the people. In response to their prayers, God has gone down to the Sanhedrin in Babylonia and comforted the people by bringing them out of exile through the actions of Cyrus, Ezra, Nehemiah, Zerubbabel bar Shealtiel, and the elders of Judah. The people then rebuilt the Temple, and they appointed priests to offer the sacrifices and Levites to guard the holy word. God sent a fire down from heaven and favorably received the sacrifices and the incenses that were offered. Like a person who provides delicacies for a beloved child, so God has provided for Israel. And like a person gathering roses from the field, God has gathered the people from Babylonia.

Rashi follows the *Targum* in his reading the verse as God's directive to the Jewish people to rebuild the Temple. Specifically, the "spice bed" is the incense offered in the Temple and "picking lilies" is the ingathering of the exiles. Ibn Ezra, however, takes the verse more literally as the young woman's statement upon awakening after having made love. He further argues that the first clause suggests God ascending to heaven and the last clause God dwelling with the angels—the righteous ones.

ו:ג אֲנִי לְדוֹדִי וְדוֹדִי לִי הָרֹעֶה בַּשׁוֹשַׁנִּים:

6:3 I AM MY BELOVED'S AND MY BELOVED IS MINE, THE ONE WHO GRAZES IN THE LILIES.

It is difficult to determine whether this is a statement of triumph or part of a continuing fantasy by the young woman who is in love. Perhaps she and her lover have achieved the ultimate union of a couple in the climax of the sexual act, in which one becomes the other. The first part of this verse has become well-known as the text that many have engraved in their wedding rings, calligraphed on their *ketubot*, and spoken or sung at their weddings. It also has been used often to describe the relationship between the individual and God. Becoming one with the other is the goal of spiritual union, as well. We want to become one with God, nearly losing ourselves in the Divine.

The *Targum* continues its ongoing allegory, reading the verse as the statement of Israel: they will worship God, whom they love, who loves them, who has restored the Divine Presence among them, and who provides them with all kinds of delights. Rashi reads the verse as Israel's response to the nations: Israel needs no help in finding God; God is with Israel. "Grazes in the lilies" suggests to Rashi that no other people have a claim on Jerusalem. Here Ibn Ezra follows the *Targum*, taking the first clause as Israel's proclamation that "we are God's and God is ours."

ו:ד יָפָה אַתְּ רַעְיָתִי כְּתִרְצָה נָאוָה כִּירוּשָׁלָם אֲיֻמָּה כַּנִּדְגָּלוֹת:

6:4 O MY DARLING, YOU ARE AS BEAUTIFUL AS TIRZAH, AS LOVELY AS JERUSALEM, AS AWESOME AS A ROW OF FLAGS.

The last word (*kanidgalot*) is as anticlimactic as it is difficult to translate. The root (*d-g-l*) means "flag." Hence, the passive form of this verb (*dagul*) means "distinguished, marked out, flagged." Here the word appears in the Hebrew verb form *nifal*; thus, the sense is "arrayed in flags." Koehler-Baumgartner (p. 213) translates it as a "row of flags." Since the young woman has been compared to two cities, mentioning the row of flags that might appear at its entrance or gates seems to follow this theme. The place name Tirzah may have been chosen by the author because of its resonance with the verb *tirzah* (you will desire, or wish, or receive favorably).

The *Targum* understands the verse as God's response to Israel, hearing the verb *tirzah* in the place name Tirzah: "How beautiful you are when you are willing to do My will. The Temple you built is as lovely as the first one, which Solomon, who was king in Jerusalem, built. When you were out in the wilderness in four columns, all the nations stood in awe of you." Rashi similarly reads the verse as God's response

Shir HaShirim: A Modern Commentary on The Song of Songs

to the people of Israel, explaining *kanidgalot* as a reference to the host of angels. Taking a more literal approach, Ibn Ezra interprets the word as an image of banners that adorn a military camp.

וּ:ה הָסֵבִּי עֵינַיִךְ מִנֶּגְדִּי שֶׁהֵם הִרְהִיבֻנִי שַׂעְרֵךְ כְּעֵדֶר הָעִזִּים שֶׁגָּלְשׁוּ מִן־הַגִּלְעָד׃

6:5 TURN YOUR EYES AWAY FROM ME, FOR THEY UPSET ME. YOUR HAIR IS LIKE A FLOCK OF GOATS BOUNDING DOWN GILEAD.

The exact sense of the word *hirhivuni* is difficult to ascertain. According to Koehler-Baumgartner (p. 1192), the *hifil* form of the root *r-h-v* can have the sense of "storm, assault, press," and the verb is translated here as "harry, confuse." In order to shape a more affective and idiomatic translation, we have chosen to translate it as "upset me." But despite feeling upset, the author borrows the image of the goats of Gilead from 4:1. The passage here can refer not just to lovers or goats, but also to our relationship with God. The notion of God turning away from us and hiding the divine face, prominent throughout sacred literature, is reflected in the spiritual sense of this verse.

The "eyes" in this verse, according to the *Targum*, are the Rabbis and scholars of Israel. It was they who proclaimed the sovereignty of the Divine during the exile. They established schools in Babylonia to teach Torah. In a restatement of its commentary on verse 4:1, the *Targum* asserts that their students have spoken words of truth like Jacob's children, who gathered stones and built a monument at Mount Gilead (Genesis 31:46–47). Rashi, on the other hand, explains the verse as the words that a young man says to his beautiful fiancée with whom he is deeply in love. He tells her not to look at him so that he does not lose control of himself. Rashi also makes a connection to God here, suggesting that the verse contains God's words concerning the Second Temple, in which God refused to house the Ark, the Ark cover, and the cherubim from the First Temple because God was upset by the people. Ibn Ezra explains that this "turning" of the "eyes" was predicted by David as the cessation of prophecy during the period of the Second Temple.

וּ:ו שִׁנַּיִךְ כְּעֵדֶר הָרְחֵלִים שֶׁעָלוּ מִן־הָרַחְצָה שֶׁכֻּלָּם מַתְאִימוֹת וְשַׁכֻּלָה אֵין בָּהֶם׃

6:6 YOUR TEETH ARE LIKE A FLOCK OF NEWLY SHORN SHEEP COMING UP FROM THE WASHING POOL. ALL ARE PAIRED, AND NONE IS MISSING.

This verse is an exact repetition of 4:2, which could be a matter of sloppy editing, but could also represent the redactor's desire to maintain the integrity of a group of

74

verses—even with repetition—that came together from a different source or out of popular culture. There is no particular reason for the special emphasis this verse is given over any other.

Departing from the commentary it provided on 4:2, the *Targum* here explains "teeth" as the priests and Levites who ate the sacrifices that were offered in the Temple and also the flocks that Jacob brought across the Jabbok ford (Genesis 32:23–24).

In his comment on 4:2, Rashi explained the verse literally as referring to a young woman. Here he explains the verse figuratively. The "teeth" are the officers and warriors of the people. The "sheep" are the righteous members of the people, for just as every part of a sheep can be used for a sacred purpose (e.g., the flesh for sacrifice and the horns for making shofars), so every act of the righteous can have a sacred purpose. Ibn Ezra also reads "teeth" as a reference to warriors.

וּ:ז כְּפֶלַח הָרִמּוֹן רַקָּתֵךְ מִבַּעַד לְצַמָּתֵךְ:

6:7 YOUR FOREHEAD ABOVE YOUR VEIL IS LIKE A SLICE OF POMEGRANATE.

This verse already appeared as the last half of 4:3. The repetition adds little to the impact of the poem in this chapter. Nor does the image appeal to us, even when we note that the pomegranate is a symbol of fertility, because of its numerous seeds. However, the *Targum* finds new meaning in the verse, suggesting that it refers to the Hasmoneans, specifically to Mattathias, the High Priest, and his sons, who were as replete with the fulfillment of the commandments as a pomegranate is filled with seeds. Ibn Ezra notes only that "your veil" is a reference to the priests.

וּ:ח שִׁשִּׁים הֵמָּה מְלָכוֹת וּשְׁמֹנִים פִּילַגְשִׁים וַעֲלָמוֹת אֵין מִסְפָּר:

6:8 THERE ARE SIXTY QUEENS AND EIGHTY CONCUBINES AND YOUNG WOMEN WITHOUT NUMBER.

The image of multitude in this verse sets up a contrast with the uniqueness presented in the next. The *Targum* connects the verse to a particular historic event—when the Greeks, led by Alexander, gathered together sixty kings descended from Esau, dressed in armor and riding on horses, and eighty dukes descended from Ishmael, riding on elephants, plus countless others, who joined to wage war against Jerusalem.

Rashi reads the verse symbolically. He takes the "sixty" as a reference to Abraham and his immediate descendants and the "eighty" as a reference to Noah and his sons and grandsons. "Young women without number" recalls all the families descended from Noah and Abraham.

ו:ט אַחַת הִיא יוֹנָתִי תַמָּתִי אַחַת הִיא לְאִמָּהּ בָּרָה הִיא לְיוֹלַדְתָּהּ
רָאוּהָ בָנוֹת וַיְאַשְּׁרוּהָ מְלָכוֹת וּפִילַגְשִׁים וַיְהַלְלוּהָ:

6:9 MY DOVE IS UNIQUE. [SHE IS] MY PERFECT ONE.
THE ONLY CHILD OF HER MOTHER, THE DARLING
OF THE ONE WHO BORE HER. GIRLS CONSIDER HER
FORTUNATE, QUEENS AND CONCUBINES PRAISE HER.

The translation of *vayash'ruha* as "consider her fortunate" follows Koehler-Baumgartner (p. 97).

The *Targum* reads the verse as a reference to the congregation of Israel when it serves God with a single heart, holds fast to the Torah, and fulfills the commandments. Then the merit of Israel is as bright as on the day on which they went forth from Egypt. Such a moment occurred when the Hasmoneans, led by Mattathias, together with all the people of Israel, went out to battle to defend Jerusalem. God gave them victory, and seeing this, all who dwelled in the area praised them, and the leaders of the kingdoms applauded them.

Rashi sees the verse as the words of a lover describing his beloved. In a more figurative comment, he takes the verse to refer to those groups of people who resolve conflicts by careful study, to Jacob and his descendants, and to the praise given to Israel by the nations of the world. In a linguistic comment, Ibn Ezra asserts that *achat* means "unique."

ו:י מִי־זֹאת הַנִּשְׁקָפָה כְּמוֹ־שָׁחַר יָפָה כַלְּבָנָה בָּרָה כַּחַמָּה אֲיֻמָּה
כַּנִּדְגָּלוֹת:

6:10 WHO IS GLIMPSED LIKE THE MORNING STAR, WHO IS
AS FAIR AS THE MOON, AS BRIGHT AS THE SUN, AS
AWESOME AS A ROW OF FLAGS?

Although *shachar* usually means "dawn," it can also mean "morning star" (Koehler-Baumgartner, p. 1467). Because of the references to two other heavenly bodies in this verse, we have chosen the latter in our translation. In this verse, one can see a progression of the intensity of light and its sources, from the dim light of the morning star to the greater light of the moon, to the still greater light of the sun. Following Koehler-Baumgartner (p. 213), we have translated *k'nidgalot* here, as we did in 6:4 where it also appeared, as "a row of flags." Such a row is an awesome sight for the onlooker, in part because of the large number of people required to hold them.

The *Targum* understands the verse as an imagined response of various nations to the deeds of the Jewish people. This is a people that rises early to perform the commandments, whose young men are as bright as the moon, and whose mature men are as desired as the sun. Their accomplishments are awe-inspiring to the inhabitants of the entire world: even when they went out into the wilderness, they did so in four columns.

Rashi reads *shachar* as "dawn." Just as the light at dawn gets gradually brighter, so did the fortunes of Israel gradually increase in the time of the Second Temple. At first subjugated and then finally victorious, the Jewish people suffered and then succeeded against the Persians and the Greeks. *K'nidgalot*, regardless of its specific translation, expresses God's praise for the people, their rulers, and their warriors.

וּיא אֶל־גִּנַּת אֱגוֹז יָרַדְתִּי לִרְאוֹת בְּאִבֵּי הַנָּחַל לִרְאוֹת הֲפָרְחָה הַגֶּפֶן הֵנֵצוּ הָרִמֹּנִים:

6:11 DOWN TO THE NUT GARDEN I WENT, TO SEE THE SHOOTS OF THE DATE PALM, TO SEE IF THE VINES HAD BLOSSOMED, IF THE POMEGRANATES WERE IN BLOOM.

Although translating this verse, like so many others in this text, presents some difficulties, a general understanding of the verse and its imagery is clear. As we have seen in 4:12 and 5:1, a "garden" can be a euphemism for pudendum. Read in this way, entering the garden is a euphemism for sexual intercourse. Perhaps the author is telling the reader, possibly with a sense of bravado, that he has once again made love to his beloved. It seems strange, though, that he has specified the garden as a "nut garden." Moreover, *ibei hanachal* is also challenging to translate. Koehler-Baumgartner (p. 2) suggests that *eiv* (singular of *ibei*) is "a shoot," or a plant still growing in the ground, while *nachal* here means "date palm" (p. 687), rather than "wadi" or "valley," as it is more commonly translated. This particular translation is preferred here because the remainder of the verse deals with specific plants, such as "nut," "vine," and "pomegranate." These may be images for the male sex organ, perhaps in its erect state.

According to the *Targum*, this verse contains God's statement about the Second Temple, which was rebuilt under the rule of Cyrus, by the Jews encouraged by Haggai and Zerubbabel. With these words, God is saying, "I have set My Presence there so that I might see the achievements of My people and to see whether the Sages—who are compared to vines and palm fronds—are as filled with good deeds as pomegranates [are filled with seeds]."

Rashi follows the *Targum* and reads the verse as God stating, "I have come into the Second Temple to see the freshness [literally, "the moisture"] of good deeds; to see 'if the vines had blossomed' [that is, if scholars have come forth from the people]; and to see the pomegranates [that is, if there are many who do good deeds]." Rashi adds that just as a nut needs to be planted in dirt, so the Jewish people had to be sent into Babylonian exile in order to develop properly. Ibn Ezra looks at the verse grammatically and suggests two different derivations for the word *eiv* (shoot), either from *abuach* (spring) or from *av* (father).

77

וּ:יב לֹא יָדַעְתִּי נַפְשִׁי שָׂמַתְנִי מַרְכְּבוֹת עַמִּי־נָדִיב:

6:12 BEFORE I KNEW IT, MY DESIRE SET ME UPON THE
CHARIOTS OF AMMI-NADIB.

This verse is also difficult to understand, but for reasons dissimilar to the previous verse. Who is Ammi-nadib, and what is his relation to the verse? Although the name Amminadab is widely known (see, for example, Exodus 6:23; Numbers 1:7, 2:3; Ruth 4:19; and I Chronicles 2:10), the name Ammi-nadib is found only here in the Bible. Koehler-Baumgartner (p. 844) suggests that the word is a proper noun meaning "my father's brother is generous." To make matters more complicated, some manuscripts of the Song of Songs have "Amminadab" in place of "Ammi-nadib" (see *Biblia Hebraica,* p. 1208). It may be that the word or name is a composite of two words: *ami* (my people) and *nadiv* (generous). This explanation would yield "my generous people," but it doesn't aid in better understanding the verse. Such an explanation does not provide an easy answer to why the woman's "desire" (or "fancy") would place her among "chariots." Perhaps she wanted to be among the men who drove the chariots. Or maybe it was a favorite place of fantasy to enjoy sexual relations. That might also explain why the verse contains a change from a masculine narrator to a feminine narrator.

None of these concerns are reflected in the commentary of the *Targum*. It takes the first words *lo yadati* (literally, "I did not know") to be the words of God, who had not previously acknowledged that among the people were to be found examples of righteousness and observance. In response, God said, "No longer will I afflict them or attempt to destroy them. Rather, I will direct Myself to benefit them. Moreover, by virtue of the presence among them of those righteous persons, who may be compared to Abraham, their progenitor, I will place them upon the chariots of kings."

Rashi understands *lo yadati* to be the words of the people of Israel. They lament that they did not know enough to keep themselves far from sin and thereby retain their glory. Rather, as the Rabbis taught, the Jewish people in the period of the Hasmoneans became mired in controversy and stumbled into senseless hatred *(sin-at chinam)*. This enabled the Roman Empire to enter their territory and enslave the people. Thus, the people's sinful desire caused them to be carried off in the chariots of other nations. Ibn Ezra explains *lo yadati* as the young woman's words as she marvels at how fast she was joined with her beloved. He suggests that *ami* and *nadiv* are really two words, noting also that some hold the letter *yod* in *ami-nadiv* to be extraneous.

Cyrus

Cyrus the Great became king of Persia around 558 B.C.E. In 539 B.C.E., Babylonia surrendered to Cyrus without going to war. His empire included Syria and the Land of Israel. When Babylonia conquered Judea in 586 B.C.E., the majority of the population was deported to Babylonia. In 537 B.C.E., Cyrus permitted the return of the Jewish people to Judea. As a result, the Jewish people considered Cyrus a messenger of God.

Ezra

Ezra was a priest who returned to Jerusalem under Zerubbabel. More of a teacher (known in the tradition as a scribe) than a priest, he led the second group of returnees from Babylonian exile. He may have been responsible for collecting and editing a large portion of the Torah as we know it. According to Nehemiah 8:3, Ezra assembled the entire community and read the Torah aloud to them. As a result, a great religious awakening ensued. The Book of Ezra records the events at the end of the Babylonian exile. The Books of Ezra and Nehemiah were once considered a single volume.

Nehemiah

Nehemiah was governor of Judea and sought to restore the orderly administration of public worship. He presumably remained in this position until his death in ca. 413 B.C.E. The Book of Nehemiah is dated ca. 430 B.C.E., when Nehemiah returned a second time to Jerusalem after his exile to Babylonia. The book, a continuation of the Book of Ezra, recounts the rebuilding of the wall around Jerusalem; the register found by Nehemiah of those who returned from Babylonia; the state of religious observance among the Jewish people at the time; the increase in the number of Jerusalem's inhabitants (including a census of the adult males and the names of the chiefs, priests, and Levites); and the dedication of the wall of Jerusalem, the arrangement of the Temple officials, and the reforms carried out by Nehemiah.

Zerubbabel

Zerubbabel (more precisely translated "Zerubavel") is mentioned in three biblical books (Haggai 1–2; Zechariah 4; and Ezra 4). On divine orders, the prophet Haggai directed Zerubbabel to begin building the Second Temple. (The building had previously stopped, and Haggai actually encouraged the continued building.) In the Book of Zechariah, God sends a message to Zerubbabel, telling him that he will succeed as a result of divine strength rather than human power. The Book of Ezra relates Zerubbabel's actual period as governor of the Jews, as well as his political activities. In the midrash, however, he is given the role of companion to the Messiah. According to the Babylonian Talmud (*Sanhedrin* 37b–38a), Zerubbabel was the son of King Jeconiah, who was taken to Babylonia during the exile by Nebuchadnezzar. This same text identifies Zerubbabel as Shealtiel. However, Ibn Ezra rejects the notion that Zerubbabel was the son of Jeconiah and suggests that he was the son of Pedaiah instead. Zerubbabel is generally identified as a son of Shealtiel. He also suggests that he was known as Sheshbazzar, which he takes as a Babylonian variant of Zerubbabel. Shealtiel, who raised Zerubbabel, was Pedaiah's brother. Zerubbabel was noted for his leadership of the Jewish people in their conflict against the Samaritans. Ibn Ezra himself was known as Bar Shealtiel because, some contend, he also had greater community status than his brother.

Tirzah

According to archaeologists, Tirzah can be identified with Tel el-Farah, a large mound located about seven miles northeast of Shechem (Nablus). Tirzah was situated at the western end of the Wadi Farah, a fertile valley that descends more than 2,000 feet over a distance of some eighteen miles. An important road through the valley connected the city with the Jordan River valley to the east, allowing Tirzah to control the travel route between the important ancient cities of Bet Shean and Shechem.

The Hasmoneans

Following the victory of Judah the Maccabee in 161 B.C.E. when full sovereignty was secured for Judea, a permanent government had to be established. Although Judah died a year after his assumption of political office, he was succeeded by his brothers Jonathan and Simeon. (Simeon's son John Hyrkanus I later succeeded Simeon and declared himself king.) This fully established the line of rule started by Simeon's father Mattathias, the High Priest.

The leaders who directly followed Judah were interested in stabilizing the area, as well as conquering territories. They succeeded in their desire to annex the Galilee region and set up effective trade relations with their neighbors.

The family was called the Hasmonean family; thus, the period in which they ruled became known as the Hasmonean period. Leaders from the generations following the rule of John Hyrkanus did not have the moral strength to rule, and a 100-year family struggle for power ensued.

Senseless Hatred (Sin-at Chinam)

Sin-at chinam is defined as the baseless hatred among Jews that destroys the very community that must observe the mitzvot. The destruction of the ancient Temple in Jerusalem is attributed to *sin-at chinam*. The Babylonian Talmud asks, "Why was the Temple destroyed, seeing that in its time they were occupying themselves with Torah precepts and the practice of *tz'dakah*? Because therein prevailed *sin-at chinam*. This teaches that groundless hatred is considered to be a sin grave as the three sins of idolatry, sexual immorality, and bloodshed together" (*Yoma* 9b).

GLEANINGS

The Essential Ingredients of Eros, Philos, *and* Agape

Eros and *philos* are both essential ingredients for a successful marriage. Having said that, my years of rabbinic counseling have convinced me that a marriage where there is *philos* but no *eros* has a far better chance of succeeding than a marriage with *eros* but no *philos*. As important as sexual chemistry and romance are for a good marriage, a warm friendship and intimacy are even more important. And most important of all is *agape*, the selfless love that brings us to sacrifice for our spouse.

Agape is altruistic love. It is the love that Buber referred to when he spoke of an I-Thou relationship. It is unconditional love, the love that caused Jonathan to give up the kingship to rescue his friend David. *Agape* is the love the Bible refers to when it speaks of one's soul being bound up in another soul. It is love as service to the other, being and giving for the welfare of the other. It is love built on empathy. It is the love when a man or woman makes their spouse the most important commitment in their life—more important than their parents, their children, their business, even themselves.

I am convinced this kind of love does not come immediately in the rush of romance to a couple. It comes after they have established intimacy, after they have begun to build a home together. That is why I tell every couple planning a wedding, the true love comes after the marriage. *Agape* is the love Golda sang to Tevye in *Fiddler on the Roof*, "For twenty-five years I lived with him, fought with him, starved with him. For twenty-five years my bed was his, if that's not love, what is?"

Eros is the love that uplifts and electrifies us; it is inner-directed. *Philos* is the love built on mutuality and friendship. *Agape* is the love built on service to the beloved; it is outer-directed. It is the love known in Judaism as *chesed*, unselfish giving for the welfare of the other. All three kinds of love are essential ingredients for a good marriage. When they are all present, a man and a woman ought to feel truly blessed.

Michael Gold, *God, Love, Sex, and Family: A Rabbi's Guide for Building Relationships That Last*
(Northvale, NJ: Jason Aronson, 1998), 87–88

Peace in the Home

The rabbis of every generation have understood how hard it is for human beings to develop and maintain intimacy, even with those they love and those to whom they feel a bond and commitment. There is so much to negotiate. Time commitments, career goals, not to mention sharing space, friends, and family with another human being who thinks differently, feels differently, acts differently, and reacts differently, are constant challenges for contemporary couples. Fortunately, despite such challenges, relationships can grow and flourish through sharing, trusting, and understanding. Intimacy grows and deepens as two lives become intertwined.

Generations of rabbis and Jews have believed that true intimacy is linked to a home where there is *sh'lom bayit*, "peace in the home." *Sh'lom bayit* does not mean that things will always be peaceful. Rather, it means finding ways to communicate with each other that are clear and honest, that are ever conscious of and concerned with protecting each other, with not harming each other through words or actions. As long as you are together, you will be engaged in a process of trying to understand each other's needs and modes of expression, of negotiating ways to honor and respect each other's differences. These will be fundamental to your finding a sense of peace in your relationship, so that peace can pervade in your home.

Daniel Judson and Nancy Wiener, *Meeting at the Well:*
A Jewish Spiritual Guide to Being Engaged (New York: UAHC Press, 2002), 23–24

Syrian Wedding Customs

Those who view the book [Song of Songs] as a series of wedding songs, in which are reflected wedding customs...in modern Syria, seek to find in these lines the representation of a special wedding ceremony. This ceremony is known in Syria as the sword-dance. On the evening of her wedding day, the Syrian bride, brandishing a sword in one hand and waving a handkerchief with the other, performs a special dance, in bare feet, by a lighted fire; while the relatives and friends, arrayed in parallel lines on both sides of the bride, sing in chorus a *wasf*, a song in praise of the bride's physical charms.

Aside from the internal difficulties this whole theory creates, necessitating a change of text in many places...it is inconceivable that an ancient Jewish practice, such as this sword-dance purports to be, could have survived in modern Syria without leaving a trace of it in Jewish life and literature.

Israel Bettan, *The Five Scrolls: A Commentary* (Cincinnati: UAHC Press, 1950), 34

The Natural Flow of Love

At the root of all the desires we may have for money, fame or meaningful relationships is the pure and simple desire of the soul to love and be known. In order to love freely and purely, we must remove the obstacles that block us from being in touch with our true essence. This is not so simple. We have to break down the walls we have constructed to protect ourselves from being hurt by other people. We have to let go of our fears and allow ourselves to be open and vulnerable. Love asks us to transcend our ego and sense of separateness and self-importance, to become giving and expanded rather than selfish and limited. Kabbalah teaches that the main challenge we have in life is to transform the desire to receive for ourselves into the desire to share with others. This challenge confronts us daily in all our interactions with others. Am I going to open my heart and let the natural flow of love come through me or will I block it with self-absorbed concerns and fears?

Melinda Ribner, *New Age Judaism: Ancient Wisdom for the Modern World*
(Deerfield Beach, FL: Simcha Press, 2000), 125

Twoness

Before separation, Adam was an undifferentiated self. After separation, a profound human desire emerges: to reunite with the "better half" while preserving the unique self. Before the separation, distance was missing. The other was absorbed in the self, swallowed without recognition of the uniqueness of the other. The new union in marriage respects the sameness and difference of the "I" and "thou." This other, like myself, is created in God's Image and is not to be made over in my own likeness. The other is not an ear into which I may shout my ambition and frustration. The other is a "thou" to be heard. The dialogue must not be turned into a soliloquy. I cannot say "thou" to myself. Marriage calls for a wisdom of love, the art to achieve the delicate balance between singularity and unity. The myth of the creation of primordial man and primordial woman out of an individual self teaches the subtle arithmetic of love: one becomes two, and two become one.

Harold Schulweis, *Finding Each Other in Judaism: Meditations on the Rites of Passage from Birth to Immortality* (New York: UAHC Press, 2001), 43–44

CHAPTER SEVEN

ז:א שׁוּבִי שׁוּבִי הַשּׁוּלַמִּית שׁוּבִי שׁוּבִי וְנֶחֱזֶה־בָּךְ מַה־תֶּחֱזוּ בַּשּׁוּלַמִּית
כִּמְחֹלַת הַמַּחֲנָיִם:

7:1 COME BACK, COME BACK, O SHULAMIT, THAT WE MAY
LOOK AT YOU. DON'T LOOK AT THE SHULAMIT, AS AT
THE *MACHANAYIM* DANCE.

Like so many other verses in this volume, this one is not easy to understand. First, the meaning of "Shulamit" is not clear. If it is a derivative of a place name (Shulam), that place has not yet been identified by scholars. Koehler-Baumgartner (p. 1482) suggests an emendation to "Shunamit," which would mean "the woman from Shunam," a place that has been identified. Second, the question of why the woman should "come back" is equally unclear, since the author has not told us previously that she has gone anywhere. Third, as we will see in 7:2, the particle *mah* can mean "don't" as well as "why." There may be some missing verses that would account for her travel elsewhere, but we have no evidence of such verses. Therefore, it is not clear whether *mah techezu* should be translated as "don't look" or "why look." Another problem is that the meaning of *kim'cholat hamachanayim* is difficult to discern. Although Koehler-Baumgartner (p. 569) translates it as "like a dance in two lines," the two words might also be translated as "like the dance of two camps." There is one variant manuscript that reads *bim'cholat,* "in the dance of," rather than "like the dance of." The author is probably suggesting some kind of line dance with which the original audience of this text would have been familiar.

For the *Targum*, the verse contains no difficulties. The people of Israel are the Shulamit, being asked to return to Jerusalem, where they will receive instruction in the Torah and proper prophecy from those who are the true prophets. The false prophets are asked why they misled the people with false prophecy that stirred up dissension and profaned the sanctity of the encampments of Israel and Judah.

Rashi takes the word *shuvi,* "turn back," as "turn away." In his reading, this statement represents the attempt by the nations to persuade Israel to turn away from God. Shulamit is their praise of Israel: "You who are perfect [or complete] in your faith [*shulamit* derived from *shaleim,* "complete"] now turn to us and we will treat you favorably, granting you power and dominion." Israel (the camps, *machanayim*) responds, "Nothing you are able to promise could match what we already had in the wilderness." Ibn Ezra also derives Shulamit from *shaleim* but relates it to Jerusalem. He connects the "dance" to the use of various musical instruments and "two camps" to two rows of dancers.

ז:ב מַה־יָּפוּ פְעָמַיִךְ בַּנְּעָלִים בַּת־נָדִיב חַמּוּקֵי יְרֵכַיִךְ כְּמוֹ חֲלָאִים
מַעֲשֵׂה יְדֵי אָמָּן:

7:2 HOW BEAUTIFUL ARE YOUR FEET IN SANDALS, O
DAUGHTER OF A PRINCE. YOUR ROUNDED THIGHS
ARE LIKE ORNAMENTS, THE HANDIWORK OF AN ARTIST.

This verse continues the context established by the first verse. The woman under
scrutiny is perhaps a great—even seductive—dancer. She either has beautiful legs or is
"light on her feet." Thus, it may be better to translate *f'amayich* as "your steps,"
rather than "your feet," although Koehler-Baumgartner (p. 952) offers either choice
as acceptable.

The *Targum* interprets "your feet" as part of a statement by Solomon delivered
through the spirit of prophecy: "How beautiful are the feet of Israel as they come to
Jerusalem, three times a year, to appear before *Adonai*, at the Pilgrimage Festivals
to offer their sacrifices. Their children, the product of their loins ["thighs"], are as
beautiful as the jewels in the crown made by Bezalel for Aaron, the High Priest."

For Rashi, the verse is praise of Israel offered by the nations in honor of Israel's
celebration of the Pilgrimage Festivals. Moreover, Rashi understands God to be the
"artist" mentioned in the verse. Ibn Ezra also reads "feet" as a reference to the Three
Pilgrimage Festivals, noting additionally that some commentators interpret the words
chamukei y'reichayich (your rounded thighs) as a reference to the hip joint.

ז:ג שָׁרְרֵךְ אַגַּן הַסַּהַר אַל־יֶחְסַר הַמָּזֶג בִּטְנֵךְ עֲרֵמַת חִטִּים סוּגָה
בַּשּׁוֹשַׁנִּים:

7:3 YOUR NAVEL IS A GOBLET, NEVER LACKING WINE. YOUR
BELLY IS LIKE A HEAP OF WHEAT FENCED IN WITH LILIES.

The poetic imagery with which the author continues to describe his lover's beauty
and sexuality can be difficult for contemporary readers to fully appreciate. Even for
those wanting to mine the text for spiritual insights and apply them to our relationship
with the Divine, these images are hard to grasp. But a basic understanding of the text
requires that the translator decide. Therefore, we have translated the word *hamazeg*
(literally, "the mixture") as "wine," because wine in the ancient world was a mixture
of syrup diluted with water. The discussion of lilies from 2:1 applies here as well.

The *Targum* understands the verse to refer to the head of the academy, by whose
merit the whole world is sustained. The description of the young woman's body is a
different kind of metaphor for Rashi, one that describes the beauty of her good deeds.
Just as all of us require "wheat" to live, so all who know the young woman become
dependent on her goodness. Taking *shoshanim* as "roses," Rashi suggests that
"bounded by roses" is a metaphor for the woman's self-control. However much
she wants to engage in sexual intercourse, she refrains, because she still sees a drop
of menstrual blood and, according to traditional Jewish law, women who are

85

menstruating are not permitted to engage in lovemaking. Ibn Ezra explains *shar'reich* as "navel" in a figurative manner. He contends that it refers to the Sanhedrin, the "center" of the community.

ז:ד שְׁנֵי שָׁדַיִךְ כִּשְׁנֵי עֳפָרִים תָּאֳמֵי צְבִיָּה:

7:4 Your two breasts are like two fawns, twins of a gazelle.

Though the image may seem strange to our modern ears, the author is continually complimenting the physical beauty of the female lover. Other than the words *haro-im bashoshanim*, "who feeds among the lilies," which is absent here, this verse is a repetition of 4:5. The *Targum* takes the "two breasts" of the verse as a reference to the two Messiahs who will deliver the people of Israel in the future. One comes from the line of David, and the other comes from the line of Ephraim (see chapter 4). The two Messiahs resemble Moses and Aaron (as in the *Targum*'s earlier interpretation), who were compared to the "twins of a gazelle." Commenting on this verse, Rashi repeats his interpretation of *shadayich* as a reference to Moses and Aaron and adds that the word also refers to the two tablets of the Decalogue.

ז:ה צַוָּארֵךְ כְּמִגְדַּל הַשֵּׁן עֵינַיִךְ בְּרֵכוֹת בְּחֶשְׁבּוֹן עַל־שַׁעַר בַּת־רַבִּים
אַפֵּךְ כְּמִגְדַּל הַלְּבָנוֹן צוֹפֶה פְּנֵי דַמָּשֶׂק:

7:5 Your throat is like a tower of ivory. Your eyes are like pools in Heshbon, near the Bath-rabbim gate. Your nose is like a tower in Lebanon that faces Damascus.

While the places mentioned in the verse must have suggested meaningful comparisons to the poet and the intended audience of the Song of Songs, the comparisons are no longer clear to most modern readers.

The *Targum* suggests that the verse is a reference to the *av beit din*, the second in command of the Sanhedrin, who had sufficient power to impose his rule upon the people and could even compel the payment of taxes by inflicting lashes. The *Targum* also calls our attention to a similar course of action taken by King Solomon, who built a tower of ivory and forced the people of Israel to support the enterprise.

Rashi understands the "throat" as the Temple and its altar. For him, the "eyes" refer to the Sages, and the "Bath-rabbim gate" refers to the Sanhedrin. Basing his comment on Isaiah 3:9, Rashi suggests that the description of the young woman's face is a metaphor for her spiritual condition. Ibn Ezra also interprets the verse figuratively: "your throat" refers to the messianic king, "your eyes" are the prophets, and "your nose" refers to the High Priest.

זּו רֹאשֵׁךְ עָלַיִךְ כַּכַּרְמֶל וְדַלַּת רֹאשֵׁךְ כָּאַרְגָּמָן מֶלֶךְ אָסוּר בָּרְהָטִים:

7:6 THE HEAD UPON YOU IS LIKE CRIMSON. YOUR HAIR IS
LIKE PURPLE. A KING IS TRAPPED IN YOUR TRESSES.

This is another difficult verse, with images that are unclear and strange to the modern reader. One difficulty lies in the word *karmel*. This may be the place name "Carmel" as in Mount Carmel, it may be vocalized as *karmil*, meaning "crimson" (Koehler-Baumgartner, p. 499), or it may mean "orchard." To add to this difficulty, the word *alayich* (literally, "upon you, for you") is apparently extraneous. Translating *karmel* as "crimson" in the first clause sets up a parallel to the second clause: the color purple. However, such a solution does not take into account the word *alayich*. If *karmel* is translated as "orchard," then *alayich* could be related to *aleh*, meaning "shoot" or "foliage" (Koehler-Baumgartner, p. 831). The three words of the clause would then read "your head, your foliage is like an orchard" and could be a description of a full head of hair. Following this translation, the "purple" of the second clause could suggest richness rather than a color. Simply put, perhaps this verse could be read as "you have a good head of hair."

The *Targum* is untroubled by the difficulties with a literal reading of the verse. For the *Targum*, the "head" is the king, who is as righteous as Elijah the Prophet, who worked zealously for God, slew the false prophets at Mount Carmel, and moved the Israelites back to their worship of God. Understanding *dalat* (hair) as *dalut* (poverty), the *Targum* continues: "...the people now poor will in the future put on purple, as Daniel and Mordecai did. The merit of the two derived from the merit of Abraham; and of Isaac, whose father bound him; and also of Jacob, who peeled a staff in the watering troughs." This idea of the merit of Jacob that the *Targum* raises is a play on the word *rahatim* (troughs), which is discussed in Koehler-Baumgartner (pp. 1193–94).

Rashi has a completely different interpretation of this verse, explaining that *karmel* refers to the *t'fillin*. *Alayich* refers to the name of God, which is "upon you." *Dalat rosheich* (your hair) is a reference to the Nazirites, who, as part of their oath, did not cut their hair. The "king" also refers to the name of God. "Trapped" may refer to God's love for the Jewish people because they run to observe the commandments (a play on the root *resh-hei-tav*). Ibn Ezra, however, takes *karmel* to refer to the color crimson. He also reads "head" as an allusion to Nehemiah, "hair" to Elijah, and "king" to the Messiah.

זּו מַה־יָּפִית וּמַה־נָּעַמְתְּ אַהֲבָה בַּתַּעֲנוּגִים:

7:7 HOW BEAUTIFUL, HOW DELICIOUS IS LOVE IN ALL ITS
DELIGHTS.

Whether this is a statement about the delights of love in general or this loved woman in particular, the word "all" seems to encompass the sexuality described throughout the book. However, this verse can also be easily read as a description of divine love: how wonderful indeed is divine love in all of its facets.

The *Targum* claims that the verse speaks of King Solomon praising the Israelite community for having lovingly taken on the "yoke of the commandments," the responsibility to live according to the mitzvot. This is the lover now making a general statement about the beauty of his beloved, according to Rashi, having previously described her in detail. Ibn Ezra notes that there is nothing in life as delightful as sexual desire. He also takes the verse as a reference to Israel's restoration to greatness. For Gersonides, the verse reminds us that the knowledge of truth is our ultimate desire. For "those who know the truth," there is no bodily pleasure that can compare.

ז:ח זֹאת קוֹמָתֵךְ דָּמְתָה לְתָמָר וְשָׁדַיִךְ לְאַשְׁכֹּלוֹת:

> 7:8 YOUR STATURE IS LIKE A PALM TREE. YOUR BREASTS
>   ARE LIKE CLUSTERS.

The lover returns to describing the beauty of the one he loves. For the *Targum*, this verse relates to the priests who bless the people. Their outstretched hands are like the fronds of a palm tree. When they prostrate themselves with their faces pressed to the ground, their faces are like clusters of grapes.

Rashi takes the verse as a reference to the beauty of the people during the reign of Nebuchadnezzar, when Israel alone stood erect as others bowed down to idols. For him, the "breasts" refer to Daniel, Hananiah, Mishael, and Azariah, whose teachings nourished the Jewish people. Similarly, Ibn Ezra takes "stature" to refer to a vine. He understands the word as a reference to the moral stature of the people.

ז:ט אָמַרְתִּי אֶעֱלֶה בְתָמָר אֹחֲזָה בְּסַנְסִנָּיו וְיִהְיוּ־נָא שָׁדַיִךְ כְּאֶשְׁכְּלוֹת
הַגֶּפֶן וְרֵיחַ אַפֵּךְ כַּתַּפּוּחִים:

> 7:9 I SAY [TO MYSELF] LET ME CLIMB THE PALM. LET ME
>   GRAB ITS BRANCHES. LET YOUR BREASTS BE CLUSTERS
>   OF GRAPES, AND LET THE SMELL OF YOUR MOUTH BE
>   LIKE APPLES.

The speaker seems eager to encounter his lover sexually. For the *Targum*, however, this verse expresses God's intention to test Daniel by seeing whether he could withstand trials as Abraham had. Comparing Abraham in this verse to a palm frond, the *Targum* reminds us that Abraham withstood ten trials. Following the trial of Daniel, God proceeded to test Hananiah, Mishael, and Azariah. If they all could pass the tests and accrue merit, then God would redeem the people of Israel, which the verse refers to as grape clusters, and their fame would waft through the world like the aroma of apples from the Garden of Eden.

Rashi also reads the verse as an expression of divine sentiment. Because of Israel's merit, God gains stature among the hosts of heaven. God is sanctified among those on earth because of Israel's steadfast dedication to the Divine Name while living among the Babylonians. Ibn Ezra notes that the word *sansinav* occurs only here in the Bible, which makes it difficult to translate properly. He adds that the "smell of your mouth" refers to the High Priest, who offers burnt offerings and incense.

ז:י וְחִכֵּךְ כְּיֵין הַטּוֹב הוֹלֵךְ לְדוֹדִי לְמֵישָׁרִים דּוֹבֵב שִׂפְתֵי יְשֵׁנִים:

7:10 YOUR MOUTH IS LIKE THE BEST WINE, FLOWING SMOOTHLY FOR MY LOVER, GLIDING DOWN THE LIPS OF THOSE ABOUT TO SLEEP.

The three clauses of this verse can be read as a dialogue: first the young man speaks to his lover, then she responds, and then they speak together. The language is reminiscent of verse 1:4. The noun *meisharim*, translated there as "rightly" or "properly," here takes on the meaning of "smoothly" (Koehler-Baumgartner, p. 578).

The *Targum* continues in its interpretation of this verse with the story of Daniel and his associates, who agree to accept the divine decree as did their ancestor Abraham, who can be compared to aged wine. They will follow the path of the prophets Elijah and Elisha, who were able to raise the dead (who might seem like those sleeping), and Ezekiel, who prophesied that the valley of the dry bones would be resurrected (Ezekiel 37).

The verse is a parable about the people of Israel, according to Rashi. "Your mouth" refers to responsa literature, and "gliding down" refers to Israel's concern that they may remain wholehearted and steadfast in their faith. Ibn Ezra takes *meisharim* to relate to good wine. He also reads "your mouth" as a reference to the poets of the people.

ז:יא אֲנִי לְדוֹדִי וְעָלַי תְּשׁוּקָתוֹ:

7:11 I BELONG TO MY BELOVED AND TOWARD ME IS HIS DESIRE.

Although *alai* (literally, "upon me") could be translated here as "toward me" (see Koehler-Baumgartner, p. 826), this is such an erotically charged verse that the literal meaning, "on me," may seem the most appropriate, as in "his desire is to be on [top of] me." In light of the later rabbinic teaching that encouraged sex between partners on Shabbat, it seems appropriate that the Rabbis also deemed this text appropriate to be read on Shabbat. The workweek was long, as were the workdays. On Shabbat, couples had a chance to relax and make love leisurely. In the context of the spirituality of Shabbat, the deed raised their physical relationship to a sacred level, something that Judaism never shied away from.

While the Rabbis made the connection between this text and its inherent sexuality, the *Targum* continues to read on a metaphoric level. For the *Targum*, the verse is a speech given by Jerusalem: "So long as I walked in the ways of the Master of the universe, God caused the Divine Presence to rest upon me. But when I turned away from God's ways, God removed the Divine Presence from me and caused me to wander among the nations." The *Targum* continues with a statement that is uncomfortable to modern ears: They ruled over me in the same manner as a man rules over his wife.

Rashi reads the verse as the response of the Jewish people to God's overtures toward them. Because of their allegiance to God, God's desire is toward them. Ibn Ezra explains that "his desire" reflects the same meaning as "your desire shall be toward your husband" (Genesis 3:16) and no one else. This is a statement of the faithfulness of the Jewish people vis-à-vis God. He explains further: "I belong to my beloved" alludes to "the portion of *Adonai* is the people" (Deuteronomy 32:9). Gersonides understands this verse as a reflection of the intellect's great desire to be in conjunction with the Active Intellect.

ז:יב לְכָה דוֹדִי נֵצֵא הַשָּׂדֶה נָלִינָה בַּכְּפָרִים׃

7:12 Come, my beloved. Let's go into the field. Let's spend the night amidst the henna plants.

The meaning of the last word, *bak'farim*, depends on whether we read the word as the plural of *k'far* (village) or of *kofar* (henna plant, as per Koehler-Baumgarter, p. 495). The context suggests the latter, as there would be no point in going into "the field" in order to end up in "the villages."

The *Targum* sees the verse as a reference to events in Israel's history. When God exiled the people to the land of Seir, the Israelites pleaded that God hear their prayers even in the cities of exile, even when they lived among the pagans.

Rashi also reads the verse as a reference to the people of Israel who lived in exile, but he offers a different suggestion as to its meaning. Rashi says that the people ask God not to judge them like city dwellers, among whom there is theft and adultery. Rather, they should be judged as those who dwell in villages, who are artisans and students of Torah. Ibn Ezra also understands the verses as a reference to the different places people live. According to him, the young woman wants to spend the night in a village and not in a big city. Then at daybreak, she wants them to go to a proper place that will have a good aroma.

זיג נַשְׁכִּימָה לַכְּרָמִים נִרְאֶה אִם־פָּרְחָה הַגֶּפֶן פִּתַּח הַסְּמָדַר הֵנֵצוּ
הָרִמּוֹנִים שָׁם אֶתֵּן אֶת־דֹּדַי לָךְ:

7:13 LET'S WAKE UP IN THE VINEYARDS. LET'S SEE IF THE
VINE HAS BUDDED, IF THE BLOSSOMS HAVE OPENED, IF
THE POMEGRANATES ARE IN BLOOM. THERE I WILL GIVE
MY CARESSES TO YOU.

This verse contains more love poetry, with its variety of erotic images framed by nature. It also creates a climate of leisure time, where the opportunity for more physical love presents itself.

The *Targum* sees the verse as the statement of the people of Israel, who say to one another that they will go early to the synagogue and to the house of study. They want to examine the Torah to see if the time has come for the people's redemption from the exile and ask the Sages whether it is time to go up to Jerusalem in order to offer up praise and sacrifice to God.

Rashi also reads the verse as an allusion to synagogues and houses of study. The "vines" are a reference to those who study the Bible. The "blossoms" are those who study the Mishnah. The "pomegranates" are those who study the Talmud. "There I will give my caresses" is Israel's promise to honor God. Ibn Ezra adds a variation to the *Targum*'s interpretation of the verse: If the people of Israel repent, they will be redeemed. If they don't repent, then God will set a cruel ruler over them with decrees as harsh as those of Haman. Then, finally, they will be redeemed.

זיד הַדּוּדָאִים נָתְנוּ־רֵיחַ וְעַל־פְּתָחֵינוּ כָּל־מְגָדִים חֲדָשִׁים גַּם־יְשָׁנִים
דּוֹדִי צָפַנְתִּי לָךְ:

7:14 THE MANDRAKES GIVE OFF FRAGRANCE, AND OVER OUR
GATES ARE ALL MANNER OF LUSCIOUS FRUITS, BOTH
FRESH AND DRIED, THAT I HAVE STORED FOR YOU, MY
BELOVED.

There is a play on words in this verse in sound and meaning. *Dodi* (my caresses) in the last clause sounds like *duda-im,* "mandrakes," which were believed to be aphrodisiacs, as the story of Reuben suggests (Genesis 30:14ff.).

For the *Targum,* this verse concerns not aphrodisiacs, but rather a promise of messianic redemption. At a time of God's choosing, God will inform the Messianic King that the time has come. The exile will then end. Like perfume, the merit of the righteous has ascended heavenward. The sages who study the words of the Scriptures within the gates of the house of study proclaim that the divine realm is at hand.

Rashi explains that *duda-im* are related to dates. He also suggests that the word implies that there are two kinds of Jews: those who are righteous and those who are wicked. At the present time, writes Rashi, both kinds of Jews seek God's presence. They can be assured that a goodly reward is stored up for them. Ibn Ezra explains that mandrakes are so named because the roots look like men (a pun which works in both English and Hebrew). In a more literal interpretation, he suggests that the young woman in the verse yearns to kiss her beloved even in public. Ibn Ezra also allows for a more figurative reading, in which the verse refers to the pious acts of our ancestors.

The Pilgrimage Festivals

Also called *shalosh r'galim* (literally, "three legs") in Hebrew, the Pilgrimage Festivals are those, Sukkot, Pesach, and Shavuot, for which Israelites made pilgrimage on foot to Jerusalem. According to the Torah, every male Israelite was required to make a pilgrimage "to the place where *Adonai* your God will choose," later identified as Jerusalem. There pilgrims offered sacrifices and brought with them a second tithe of their produce, which had to be consumed in Jerusalem. This aspect was particularly important, since the three Festivals were agricultural holidays. Pesach celebrated the barley harvest; Shavuot came at the end of the barley harvest, the beginning of the wheat harvest, and the time of the first ripe fruits; and Sukkot fell at the time of the final gathering of the crops. Each holiday also had historical significance that dominated its celebration. With the return to living in the Land of Israel, the agricultural issues regained their importance.

Head of the Academy

The head of the academy, *rosh yeshivah* in Hebrew, is the head of the institution devoted to the study of the Talmud. The term was used for *yeshivot* in the Land of Israel, beginning with the academy at Yavneh following the destruction of the Second Temple. In Babylonia, the Aramaic equivalent, *reish m'tivta*, appeared and eventually found its way into parts of the traditional liturgy, such as the *Y'kum Purkan* prayer (recited on Shabbat after the haftarah reading). In Europe, the head of the academy was often looked to for decisions in matters of community law.

Heshbon

According to the Torah, King Sihon gathered all of his people and made war with the Israelites, but the Israelites defeated him by the sword and took rule of his land. The Israelites settled in all of the cities of the Amorites—Heshbon and all of its daughter cities (Numbers 21:23–28). Heshbon, one of the most fortified cities of its time, represented the first victory of the Israelites as they entered the Land.

Elijah the Prophet and Mount Carmel

Elijah, a Hebrew prophet who dates from the ninth century B.C.E., prophesied in the Northern Kingdom of Israel. He appears in the narrative of I Kings (chapters 18–19; 21) and II Kings (chapters 1–2) during the reigns of Kings Ahab, Ahaziah, and Jehoram. Among the various events that characterized his life as a prophet, Elijah is best known for his contest with 450 prophets of Baal and 400 prophets of Asherah, who challenged him on Mount Carmel. All of the prophets, including Elijah, built altars on the mountain and invited their deities to ignite their sacrifices as evidence of their divine power. The prophets of Baal received no response to their request. After Elijah poured water on the altar, an effort to make the test even more difficult and meaningful, he called on God, whose fire consumed the entire altar.

GLEANINGS

Finding a Soul Mate

Everyone yearns to find a soul mate. As you nurture a relationship with your own soul, you become more open to attracting a soul mate. The kabbalists believe that before a soul is born into this world, it is complete in itself. A complete soul is androgynous, both male and female. Yet in order to enter this world, the soul splits in two. The male and female are disengaged from each other, enter the soul of the universe, and are clothed in their independent bodies to fulfill the tasks for which they were born. As each person grows in him- or herself and refines his or her own soul, he or she is more apt to recognize and attract the other.

Shoni Labowitz, *Miraculous Living: A Guided Journey in Kabbalah through the Ten Gates of the Tree of Life* (New York: Simon and Schuster, 1996), 280

Two Meant to Be One

The joining of the two sides will return us to the unity experienced at the beginning of creation in the Garden, when there was no distinction between male and female, Divine and human, good and evil. The world is not meant to witness eternally the separation between the two sides. This is clear from the words of our creation passage: "The Lord God said: 'It is not good *(lo tov)* for man to be alone'" [Gen. 2:18]. It indeed is not good for Adam to be alone, to stand apart from Eve, his other "side." The fragmented primal unity is not pleasing in God's eyes. This is brought home by the words *lo tov* (not good) that stand in tension with the phrase uttered by God following the creation of Adam and Eve in Chapter One [of the book of Genesis]: "And God saw all that God had made and it was very good *(tov me'od).*" You will recall that in this first Creation story, God made the human being in God's own image—unified; both male and female in one ("male and female God created them" [Gen. 1:31]). The human being can only be considered "very good" if the two opposing sides are joined together as one.

Norman Cohen, *Self, Struggle and Change: Family Conflict Stories in Genesis and Their Healing Insights for Our Lives* (Woodstock, VT: Jewish Lights, 1995), 29

Understanding the ''I''

The ''I'' is better understood in relationship than in aloneness. I know myself better when I am with another. In the face-to-face encounter with the other, the ''I'' of each partner is revealed. The critical preposition of the ''I'' is ''with.'' How am I with the other's joy and with the other's sadness? How am I with the other's health and with the other's illness? How am I with the other's triumph and with the other's failure?

The Image of God is burnished through relationship. In relationship, responsibility, compassion, feeling, and respect are exhibited and verified. Godliness is experienced through attachment with an other. Martin Buber accounts for this connection when he asks, ''Would you believe? Then love.''

Harold Schulweis, *Finding Each Other in Judaism: Meditations on the Rites of Passage from Birth to Immortality* (New York: UAHC Press, 2001), 44

Bodies, Selves

Judaism extols the body that has been given to us like priestly garb, ''for glory and for beauty.'' It does not have the made-up beauty of the marketplace, but beauty shaped by labor and by love.

Our bodies are a genuine expression of who we really are. A worker's gnarled knuckles can be beautiful; wrinkles are not ugly; hair that is thinned or streaked with gray is no disgrace. These are the badges of aging. They speak to us of the ordinary heroism of ordinary people who show up for life each day, who help a neighbor, who do an honest job, who spend a quiet evening at home.

The Rabbis so revered the real body of real people that they imbued it with the sanctity that typified priestly vestments. They prohibited tattoos, for instance, and banned self-laceration. They forbade autopsies, teaching that even a corpse should be treated with dignity, washed clean and laid gently to its eternal earthly rest.

We follow all these rules because bodies are the priestly garb for all of us, since we are made in God's image. Our bodies are given ''for glory and for beauty''—not the glory of eternal youth or the beauty of the sexy look, but the genuine luster that tells the tale of our lives, our work, our joys, and our struggles, and which becomes more beautiful with every passing day.

Lawrence Hoffman, ''Bodies, Selves,'' in *Sacred Intentions: Daily Inspiration to Strengthen the Spirit, Based on Jewish Wisdom*, ed. Kerry M. Olitzky and Lori Forman (Woodstock, VT: Jewish Lights, 1999), 62–63

CHAPTER EIGHT

ח:א מִי יִתֶּנְךָ כְּאָח לִי יוֹנֵק שְׁדֵי אִמִּי אֶמְצָאֲךָ בַחוּץ אֶשָׁקְךָ גַּם
לֹא־יָבֻזוּ לִי:

8:1 WOULD THAT YOU WERE MY BROTHER, WHO HAD
NURSED AT MY MOTHER'S BREASTS, FOR THEN WHEN
I MET YOU IN THE STREET, I COULD KISS YOU AND NO
ONE COULD SCORN ME.

On a literal level, the author writes as if an onlooker could not tell the difference
between a lover's kiss and a brotherly kiss. Ibn Ezra interprets the verse exactly in this
way, writing that if the woman's lover were her brother, then they could kiss in public
and not be ashamed. Metaphorically, the *Targum* takes the verse as continuing the
description of the time when the Messiah will be revealed to the people of Israel. The
people will say to the Messiah: "Be like a brother to us and let us go up to Jerusalem.
Together we will there be suckled on the meanings of Torah. While we wandered
outside the Land, we remembered God's name. We sacrificed ourselves for God. As a
result, the people of the Land did not despise us."

Rashi understands the verse as a statement of the people. In his reading, "my
brother" is a request for God to comfort them, just as Joseph comforted his brothers
who had intended him evil. He reads "met you in the street" as a reference to the
prophets who speak to the people. Were the people to repent, then no one would or
could scorn them.

ח:ב אֶנְהָגֲךָ אֲבִיאֲךָ אֶל־בֵּית אִמִּי תְּלַמְּדֵנִי אַשְׁקְךָ מִיַּיִן הָרֶקַח מֵעֲסִיס
רִמֹּנִי:

8:2 I WOULD LEAD YOU, I WOULD BRING YOU TO MY
MOTHER'S HOUSE. YOU WOULD TEACH ME. I WOULD
GIVE YOU SOME SPICED WINE AND SOME OF MY
POMEGRANATE JUICE TO DRINK.

The word *t'lam'deini* could mean either "she will teach me" or "you will teach me."
The latter seems to fit the context better.

With this verse, the *Targum* continues its discussion of the messianic time. The
people of Israel, personified in the verse as the young woman, speak to the Messiah.
Together, the people will bring the Messiah to the Temple, where he (the son of
David) will teach Israel to fear the Divine and walk in the way of God. Then all the

95

people of Israel will take part in the messianic banquet, eating the Leviathan, drinking wine stored away at Creation, and tasting the pomegranates intended for the righteous in the world-to-come.

Rashi takes "my mother's house" to be the Temple. The "wine" represents the drink offerings. "You would teach me" means "as You used to teach me in the Tent of Meeting." Rashi's view is that this phrase concerns the teaching of how to drink spiced wine.

ח:ג שְׂמֹאלוֹ תַּחַת רֹאשִׁי וִימִינוֹ תְּחַבְּקֵנִי:

8:3 WOULD THAT HIS LEFT HAND BE BENEATH MY HEAD
AND HIS RIGHT HAND EMBRACE ME.

This verse, a repetition of 2:6, is followed in 8:4 by a repetition of 2:7. It is read by the *Targum* as the response of Israel, who says, "I am the chosen from among all people, because I fasten *t'fillin* on my head and my left hand. And I affix a mezuzah on the right side of the doorpost to prevent the entrance of demons."

Rashi relates the verse to the history of the people of Israel. Repeating his comment from 2:6, he takes "left hand...beneath my head" as a reference to the Israelites being sustained in the wilderness. Ibn Ezra reads the verse as an indication that the two lovers are now together. He adds that the verse is also a reference to the evening and morning burnt offerings in the Temple.

ח:ד הִשְׁבַּעְתִּי אֶתְכֶם בְּנוֹת יְרוּשָׁלָם מַה־תָּעִירוּ וּמַה־תְּעֹרְרוּ אֶת־
הָאַהֲבָה עַד שֶׁתֶּחְפָּץ:

8:4 O DAUGHTERS OF JERUSALEM, I CHARGE YOU: DON'T
WAKE, DON'T EXCITE LOVE UNTIL IT PLEASES.

The *Targum* presents this verse as the response of the Messiah, who charges the people to resist the temptation of leaving the exile and to rebel against the armies of Gog and Magog, even though they are somewhat delayed in conquering the nations that waged war against Jerusalem. The Messiah goes on to exhort Israel, saying that soon God will remember the loving acts of the righteous and they will be redeemed by God.

Rashi understands the verse as the divine response to the people of Israel, who are not troubled by the Babylonian exile. They are not to "wake" or "excite," because such actions will not help those still in exile.

ח:ה מִי זֹאת עֹלָה מִן־הַמִּדְבָּר מִתְרַפֶּקֶת עַל־דּוֹדָהּ תַּחַת הַתַּפּוּחַ
עוֹרַרְתִּיךְ שָׁמָּה חִבְּלַתְךָ אִמֶּךָ שָׁמָּה חִבְּלָה יְלָדַתְךָ:

8:5 WHO IS COMING UP FROM THE WILDERNESS, LEANING
ON HER LOVER? BENEATH THE APPLE TREE, I AROUSED
YOU. IT WAS THERE THAT YOUR MOTHER CONCEIVED
YOU. IT WAS THERE THAT SHE WHO BORE YOU
CONCEIVED YOU.

We are presented with several difficulties as we consider why the author changes the
speaker in the middle of this verse. Perhaps the first clause is meant to be read as a
chorus of voices. It might even be an allusion to a wedding ritual, with the entrance of
the bride on the arm of the groom. The symbolism of the words "wilderness" and
"apple tree" is significant. The verb *orer* (to arouse) can mean either to arouse from
sleep or to arouse sexually.

In the *Targum*'s interpretation, the verse is a prophetic statement made by King
Solomon. He announces that those from the nations who died will rot before the
Mount of Olives, while those from the people of Israel who died will be resurrected at
the end of days. Those righteous Jews who died in the exile will move through
subterranean channels to the Land of Israel and proceed to the Mount of Olives,
where they will be resurrected. The wicked among the Israelites, although they may
have died and been buried in the Land of Israel, will be cast out of the Land the way
one throws a stone at a post. Upon observing all of this, those who dwell on earth will
ask, "By what merit can this people depart from this land by the thousands as one
might leave the wilderness and go up to the Land of Israel?" They are delivered as a
result of the same divine love that brought them to the foot of Mount Sinai to receive
the Torah. At that future time, Zion, as the mother of Israel, will bear her child, and
Jerusalem will receive the children of the exile.

In Rashi's understanding of the verse, God and those who attend to God (angels)
address this verse to the people of Israel as if to say, "How important is this people,
who came out of the wilderness with the gifts of Torah and the Divine Presence! Now
the divine love for the people of Israel is manifest even though they remain in exile."
Rashi interprets *mitrapeket* (leaning) as "joined." Thus, God affirms the connection
that God feels with the people. They are linked to the Divine. Similarly, Rashi reads
"beneath the apple tree" as a reference to the theophany at Sinai. In a more literal
interpretation, Rashi suggests that the language of this verse reflects a young woman
who wakens her lover at night by embracing and kissing him. But Rashi also suggests
that this is a metaphor for the mutual love between God and Israel. In a linguistic
comment, Ibn Ezra notes that the word *mitrapeket* occurs in the Bible only in this
verse. He adds that the Arabic word *rapaka*, meaning "to cling to," helps us with the
meaning of *mitrapeket*. While Ibn Ezra takes the verse to indicate the love that
the young woman has for her beloved, he also suggests that the verse is a reference
to the movement by Israel from Egypt into the wilderness and then to the Land.

He contends that Israel's past glory prefigures the messianic glory; for Ibn Ezra, the "beloved" is the Messiah.

ח:ו שִׂימֵנִי כַחוֹתָם עַל־לִבֶּךָ כַּחוֹתָם עַל־זְרוֹעֶךָ כִּי־עַזָּה כַמָּוֶת אַהֲבָה
קָשָׁה כִשְׁאוֹל קִנְאָה רְשָׁפֶיהָ רִשְׁפֵּי אֵשׁ שַׁלְהֶבֶתְיָה:

8:6 Set me as a seal upon your heart, as a seal upon your arm, for love is as strong as death [and] jealousy is as powerful as Sheol. Its flashes are flashes of fire, an enormous flame.

This well-known verse has lent itself to numerous musical settings, often used for weddings. The image of "a seal upon your heart" seems clearer than "a seal upon your arm." The first image suggests that the young woman asks her lover not to love another. It is unclear how the second image follows the first. Perhaps it is a request that her lover not hold another.

The notion of "Sheol" raises a question as well. The author could be referring to the grave in general—that is, death. However, Sheol is a specific place and may represent the netherworld, or *Geihinom*. The author's intent may be found in the dating of the book. The perspective seen in most of the Bible is that death is the end of human existence. For Job, death and the grave free the individual from the pain of life (Job 3:17–22). It was only in postbiblical Judaism that the Rabbis developed the notion that a painful realm might exist for some to enter following death. Perhaps the author intended to suggest that jealousy created as much pain for the living as the torments of the underworld might provide for the dead. The author's understanding of an afterlife may offer a clue to dating this text. If the author intended to suggest that pain caused by jealousy is tantamount to the pain of living in the underworld, then it could be argued that *Shir HaShirim* was written at the end of the biblical period.

Koehler-Baumgartner points out (pp. 1297–98) that neither the etymology of the word *reshef* nor the specific meanings of the words that are derived from it (*r'shafeha* and *rishpei*) are clear. It may be that the word means "fire," "blaze," or "flash." Alternatively, it may mean "arrow," as it does in Psalm 76:4. Although we are familiar with the popular image of the arrow of love in Cupid's hand, we are not accustomed to the jealously that might be directed by such arrows, as the verse suggests. As a result, we have translated *r'shafeha* and *rishpei* as "its flashes" and "flashes of" rather than as "arrow." The final challenge of the verse is the word *shalhevetyah*, which appears in the Bible only here. The word seems to be made up of two words: *shalhevet* (flame), as is attested elsewhere (Job 15:30), and *Yah*, the Divine Name. Perhaps the combination means lightning (Koehler-Baumgartner, p. 1505), or simply an enormous flame that might even be sent by God.

The *Targum* continues its exposition on the chapter as a reference to the advent of the Messiah. On that day, the Israelites, presented in this verse as a young woman, will say to their divine master, "Set me as a seal upon your heart and as a seal upon your arm, that we may never again be exiled, for [our] love of God is as strong as death." While the jealousy of the nations is as fierce as *Geihinom*, the hatred that they stored up against the Israelites may be likened to glowing coals of the fire of *Geihinom*, which God created on the second day of Creation to engulf and destroy idolaters.

Rashi's comments seem to reflect his personal experience of love. He understands the verse as a statement by the Israelites to God: "Because the love we have for You 'set [us] as a seal upon Your heart,' You don't forget us. Since our love for You is 'as strong as death,' we are slain on Your behalf. Moreover, 'jealousy is as powerful as Sheol' is a reference to the controversies in which we have engaged the nations on Your account." Rashi translates *kin-ah* (jealousy) with the Middle French *enfirement*, which he explains as the heart's commitment to vengeance. This idea may be the source of the Modern French *enfeirvement* (to become impassioned). Rashi also equates the flashes of fire to the flames of *Geihinom*.

R'shafeha is explained as "coals of fire" by Ibn Ezra, who also notes the discussion among the Masoretes as to whether the word *shalhevetyah* is one or two words. Rashi contends that it is two words, in which the last particle or word *yah* is indeed the Divine Name, as is the case with *eil* in *har'rei eil* (Psalm 36:7). Ibn Ezra explains the "seal" as a suggestion that the young woman wants to be joined to her lover's heart as closely as a *chotam*—which he takes to mean a signet ring—fits on her finger. He also takes the verse as a statement by the people of Israel, who want to be eternally linked to the Divine Presence.

ח:ז מַיִם רַבִּים לֹא יוּכְלוּ לְכַבּוֹת אֶת־הָאַהֲבָה וּנְהָרוֹת לֹא יִשְׁטְפוּהָ
אִם־יִתֵּן אִישׁ אֶת־כָּל־הוֹן בֵּיתוֹ בָּאַהֲבָה בּוֹז יָבוּזוּ לוֹ:

8:7 STREAMS OF WATER CAN'T EXTINGUISH LOVE, NOR CAN RIVERS SWEEP IT AWAY; [YET] WERE A MAN TO GIVE EVERYTHING THAT HE HAD FOR LOVE, EVERYONE WOULD MOCK HIM.

This verse continues the previous one. It is difficult to adequately match a translation to the evocative Hebrew. Having described "jealousy" as a "flame," the writer indirectly suggests that "love" is a fire by using the onomatopoeic root *kaf-bet-hei* (to put out, to quench). He then uses the root *shin-tav-fei*, which suggests the gushing or cascading of water, translated here as "sweep away." The love between two lovers is exceptionally powerful, yet true love is something that cannot be bought, regardless of the price.

The *Targum* regards the verse as a divine promise to the people of Israel. Were all the nations of the world to gather together, with all their sovereign rulers, they would not be able to remove God's love from the people of Israel, nor would they be able to destroy them. God adds a further promise: were a person in the exile to give up everything in order to acquire wisdom, that person would receive a double portion in the world-to-come and be repaid for the contempt suffered from the camp of Gog.

For Rashi, the "streams of water" are the Babylonians and the "rivers" are their nobles and kings, unable to vanquish Israel by force or persuasion. Although they expend all their wealth attempting to seduce Israel away from God, they will fail. They will be condemned by God and the members of the divine court, who will attest to Israel's loyalty to God.

Haman is Ibn Ezra's example of "a man... [who would] give everything he had" in an attempt to interfere with the love of God for Israel. In an unusually literal comment, Gersonides suggests that the author demonstrates the power of love by suggesting that it cannot be overcome by streams and rivers or bought with money.

ח:ח אָחוֹת לָנוּ קְטַנָּה וְשָׁדַיִם אֵין לָהּ מַה־נַּעֲשֶׂה לַאֲחֹתֵנוּ בַּיּוֹם שֶׁיְּדֻבַּר־בָּהּ:

8:8 WE HAVE A LITTLE SISTER WHO HAS NO BREASTS. WHAT SHALL WE DO FOR OUR SISTER WHEN IT COMES TIME TO BE SPOKEN FOR?

The context and timing of this verse make it difficult to explain. If the Song of Songs is read as a drama of sorts, then this verse seems out of place. Even if this book is understood as a collection of wedding songs, the placement of this verse is still puzzling. If being "spoken for" refers to an arranged marriage, then "speaking" is long overdue in light of the verses that have preceded this one. Moreover, the young woman who is being "spoken" about is no longer a young girl. Perhaps the author is simply reminiscing about the young woman who is the main character of the Song of Songs, remembering an earlier time when her brothers could control her—and rein in the expressions of sexual love that are woven throughout the previous chapters of this book.

The *Targum* puts the verse into the mouth of the angels. They say to one another: there is one small people on earth whose merits are few and has neither kings nor nobles who could enter into battle with Gog. What shall we do for that people when the nations of the earth speak of going into battle against her?

Following the *Targum*, Rashi also reads the verse as a statement about the people of Israel. In his explanation, based on a wordplay between the noun *achot*/sister and the verb *ichah*/unite, he adds the midrash (from *Tanchuma, Lech L'cha* 2 and elsewhere) that this people united the world. In his reading, "be spoken for" is a reference to the words of the Babylonians who plot against Israel. Ibn Ezra takes the verse to be a statement of the young woman when she was younger and her brothers, concerned about her virtue, made her a watcher of the vineyards (see 1:6). Ibn Ezra reads "spoken for" as a reference to marriage. In a more figurative interpretation, he also sees the term as a reference to the advent of the Messiah.

אִם־חוֹמָה הִיא נִבְנֶה עָלֶיהָ טִירַת כָּסֶף וְאִם־דֶּלֶת הִיא נָצוּר ח:ט
עָלֶיהָ לוּחַ אָרֶז:

8:9 IF SHE WERE A WALL, THEN WE WOULD BUILD A SILVER
BATTLEMENT FOR HER. IF SHE WERE A DOOR, THEN WE
WOULD BARRICADE HER WITH A CEDAR DOOR.

We have followed Koehler-Baumgartner (p. 1015) in translating *natzur* as "we would
barricade." It seems clear that what is being discussed here is the chastity of the
young girl. Like the previous verse, this one appears to be out of place here. Perhaps
this verse is meant to be a memory from a different time, whose main focus is the
young woman whose sexuality pervades most of the rest of the book. Alternatively, it
could be a folk saying of sorts, something similar to "locking the barn door after the
horse has escaped." We have also followed Koehler-Baumgartner (p. 374) in
translating *tirat* as "battlement [of]." The word suggests a row of stones that have
been added to the wall for reinforcement. The verse seems to suggest that if the
young woman remains chaste, her brothers will reward her with silver.

The *Targum* places the verse in the mouth of Michael, Israel's ministering angel.
If the people of Israel are destined to be a fortress among the nations, then they will
be given silver to acquire the unity of God. The other angels, their scribes, and
Michael will encircle them like rows of silver. No nation will have permission to rule
over them, just as no worm has power over silver. Even if the people of Israel were to
be deficient in the performance of mitzvot, then the angels would implore God to
have mercy upon them. They would ask God to remember the merit of the Torah
they study, to inscribe them on the tablets of God's heart like infants, and to harden
them like cedar to confront the nations.

Rashi takes the verse as a reference to the Jewish people. If they are firm in their
faith and their reverence for God, they will be like a wall of brass that is so strong it
cannot be breached. Rashi proceeds in his commentary to specify that a brass wall
means the Jews will not marry outside the group, and no one outside the group will
marry them. The reward of the "silver battlement" will be the rebuilding of Jerusalem
and the Temple. On the other hand, if the Jewish people become like a swinging
door, so that nations may enter and Jews may leave, worm-eaten boards will have to
be fastened upon them in order to make them look unattractive. Ibn Ezra understands
"wall" to mean a virgin who will be rewarded with jewelry, and "door" to signify a
sexually experienced woman who will be punished (because of outdated views
reflecting discomfort with women's sexuality) by being shut away. He also sees the
people of Israel in this verse. In this context, "wall" indicates being resolute in faith,
while "door" indicates a failure to keep the mitzvot. If the people of Israel are
steadfast, they will be rewarded by being brought into the Land of Israel during the
period of messianic redemption. If they are not, they will be prevented from entering
the Land.

ח:י אֲנִי חוֹמָה וְשָׁדַי כַּמִּגְדָּלוֹת אָז הָיִיתִי בְעֵינָיו כְּמוֹצְאֵת שָׁלוֹם:

8:10 I AM A WALL, AND MY BREASTS ARE LIKE TOWERS, SO I BECOME IN HIS EYES AS ONE WHO FINDS PEACE.

The last two words of the verse, *k'motz'eit shalom*, don't seem to make sense in this context. According to Koehler-Baumgartner (pp. 1506–10), *shalom* can have a number of meanings, including "peace," "welfare," "prosperity," and "health." The meaning of *shalom* must thus be determined in relationship to *k'motz'eit*. But the precise meaning of this word is unclear. *Motz'eit* could be the simple (or *kal* form) feminine participle of the verb *matza* (find). Or it could be the causative (*hifil* form) feminine participle of the verb *yatza* (go out), therefore meaning "bring out." Koehler-Baumgartner (p. 1509) accepts the latter explanation and translates the phrase as "to have an offer of peace issued." But since that phrase makes little sense in the context of the verse, we have translated it as "as one who finds peace," suggesting that the young woman has found her love and thereby has found peace. The midrash (*Tanchuma, Lech L'cha* 2) interprets the words differently. The author of the midrash applies verses 8:9–10 to Abraham, who unified *(ichah)* humanity and preached against idolatry. As a result, Nimrod, the idolator, cast Abraham into a fiery furnace. The fact that Abraham was saved from death is indicated by *k'motz'eit shalom* (as one who finds peace), but reading the phrase in the passive participle feminine (the *hofal* form) as *k'mutz'at shalom*, "as one brought in peace."

The *Targum* presents this verse as a response from the Israelites, saying that they are as strong as a wall, in their mastery of words of Torah, and their children as powerful as a tower. As soon as the Israelites respond, they will find God's favor and will greet all the inhabitants of the world in peace.

Rashi also sees the verse as a response from the Israelites. For him, the phrase "my breasts are like towers" refers to the synagogues and schools that suckle Israel with words of Torah. His interpretation of the last two words of the verse employs both passive and active meanings of *motz'eit*. He interprets the phrases as "a bride who is found to be *sh'leimah* [perfect] and one who finds peace at home with her spouse." Ibn Ezra understands the verse as the young woman's statement that even though she has reached puberty and has developed breasts, she is still a virgin. In Ibn Ezra's reading, "his eyes" means in the eyes of the one who suspected that she was not a virgin and now accepts that she indeed is. As a result of this change in attitude, she "has found peace." It is clear that the commentators are preoccupied with issues of virginity and the role it plays in the development of sexual identity. Ibn Ezra also interprets the verse as a statement by the Israelites: "We have kept our religion and maintained the Written and Oral Law. Thus, all of Israel can be at ease."

ח:יא כֶּרֶם הָיָה לִשְׁלֹמֹה בְּבַעַל הָמוֹן נָתַן אֶת-הַכֶּרֶם לַנֹּטְרִים אִישׁ יָבִא בְּפִרְיוֹ אֶלֶף כָּסֶף:

8:11 SOLOMON HAD A VINEYARD IN BAAL HAMON. HE PUT GUARDS IN THE VINEYARD. EACH PIECE OF FRUIT WAS WORTH A THOUSAND SILVER PIECES.

The words *ish yavi b'firyo* literally mean "a man will bring for its fruit." It is not clear who the man is. The last two words of the verse, *elef kasef*, "a thousand [pieces of] silver," suggest why guards were necessary. Therefore, by context, we have decided that the "man" is any person and have translated it as "each piece of fruit was worth a thousand silver pieces."

The *Targum* takes the verse as a reference to events in Jewish history, identifying Israel as a nation that walked in the way of the Master of the universe, the Source of peace. In this interpretation, Solomon is a metaphor for God. The Jewish nation may be compared to a vineyard. God set Jerusalem in the midst of the nation and placed over it kings from the House of David to take care of it, much as guards look after a vineyard. After Solomon died, Rehoboam succeeded him. But Jeroboam rebelled and divided the kingdom. He led away ten tribes on the advice of the powerful Ahijah of Shiloh. The *Targum* reports these events as they appear in I Kings 14–16 and II Chronicles 11–13.

Rashi identifies "vineyard" as the people of Israel and "Baal Hamon" as Jerusalem. He explains "guards" as the harsh overlords of Persia and Babylonia who exacted taxes of "a thousand silver pieces" from the people. Ibn Ezra describes Baal Hamon as a specific place that has many vineyards. He also understands "vineyard" as the people of Israel, over whom Solomon reigned as king. Thus, the "guards" are the rightful kings of Israel.

ח:יב כַּרְמִי שֶׁלִּי לְפָנָי הָאֶלֶף לְךָ שְׁלֹמֹה וּמָאתַיִם לְנֹטְרִים אֶת-פִּרְיוֹ:

8:12 I HAVE MY OWN VINEYARD. SOLOMON, YOU COULD HAVE A THOUSAND WITH TWO HUNDRED GUARDS TO WATCH THE FRUIT.

The speaker has changed once again. Now it is the young man, the lover, who speaks. The young woman, his beloved, is his vineyard. Previously (see 5:1), she was his garden.

The *Targum* continues with a discussion of Jewish history. When Solomon heard the prophecy of Ahijah of Shiloh concerning the division of the united kingdom, he wanted to kill him, but Ahijah escaped and went to Egypt. Solomon had learned through prophecy that he would rule over the ten tribes while he was alive. However, when he died, Jeroboam son of Nebat would rule over the ten tribes, and his own son Rehoboam would only rule over the two tribes of Judah and Benjamin.

Rashi relates the verse to what will happen when the Messiah comes. God will bring the Babylonians to judgment, telling them that although they were permitted to rule harshly over Israel, the Israelites are God's "vineyard" and belong only to the Divine. In reply, the Babylonians tell God that they will return to Israel whatever they have taken from them. Moreover, they will add more of their own money. They will pay for the scholars who are the "guards to watch the fruit," and they will fulfill the words of the prophet, "for her merchandise will be for those who dwell before *Adonai*" (Isaiah 23:18). It is clear that while Rashi specifies the Babylonians, he means all those who have dominion over Israel.

Ibn Ezra sees the verse as a statement by the young woman. She wants neither money nor any kind of profit; she only wants to be with her beloved. But Ibn Ezra also reads the verse as Solomon's divinely inspired statement that the Jewish people will be brought back to God's presence in the future. In his interpretation, "thousand" is the Messiah and the "two hundred" are the tribes of Judah and Benjamin.

חːיג הַיּוֹשֶׁבֶת בַּגַּנִּים חֲבֵרִים מַקְשִׁיבִים לְקוֹלֵךְ הַשְׁמִיעִינִי:

8:13 O YOU WHO SIT IN THE GARDENS, [OUR] FRIENDS CAN
HEAR YOUR VOICE. LET ME HEAR IT TOO.

The relationship between this verse and the one that precedes it is unclear. Who is being addressed, and by whom? Perhaps this is part of the poem that describes the lovers who speak in the previous verses. But who are these friends, and what is their relationship to the lovers? Taking a cue from the way nouns are used in Modern Hebrew, where "friends" implies "our friends," we have added "our" to the translation, assuming that the "friends" are surely known to the couple.

The *Targum* takes the verse as Solomon's statement at the end of his prophecy. Israel is likened to a small garden set among the nations of the world. God will say to Israel: "All of you who inhabit the study house together with the members of the Sanhedrin and obey its leader, let Me hear the words of your Torah when you sit in judgment. Then I will agree with all that you do."

Like the *Targum*, Rashi also understands the verse as God's statement to the people of Israel. However, he identifies "gardens" as all the foreign lands in which Israel has been forced to live. He reads "sit" as a reference to the synagogues and schools that exist in the Diaspora. For him, *chaverim* (friends) are the angels who want to listen to the students studying in these schools. This is in keeping with the idea expressed in Job that people sanctify the Divine Name of God: "When the morning stars sang together and all the children of God shouted for joy" (Job 38:7). Ibn Ezra understands the one "who sit[s] in the gardens" as the *Shechinah*, the Divine Presence, who is desirous of having the angels ("friends") listen to Israel's songs of praise.

ח:יד בְּרַח דּוֹדִי וּדְמֵה־לְךָ לִצְבִי אוֹ לְעֹפֶר הָאַיָּלִים עַל הָרֵי בְשָׂמִים:

8:14 QUICK NOW, MY BELOVED, PLAY THE GAZELLE OR THE
FAWN UPON THE HILLS OF SPICES.

The verse seems to be some sort of a summary, though its purpose as a conclusion
is unclear. The images of the gazelle and fawn were introduced previously, in 2:17,
but the verse may be a fragment that was not part of the original set of poems.
We assume that the young woman is speaking these final lines to her lover, but they
may be the words of a chorus. In one way or another, this young woman says to her
potential lover: "Love me quickly." The expected response, "And I will love you in
return," is missing from the verse. This is the prayer of every heart, whether the
intended lover is human or divine.

The *Targum* continues the messianic theme that it found in previous verses. At that
future date, the elders of Israel will say, "O God, quickly take Your compassion from a
defiled land and set Your Presence in heaven. When troubles come, we pray to You.
May You be like a gazelle that sleeps with one eye shut and the other eye open. May
You be like a fawn that runs while looking behind itself. May You look at us from
heaven and see our present pain and suffering. May the day come when You will
favor us, deliver us, and bring us to Jerusalem's heights, so that the priests can burn
the incense of spices before You."

Rashi explains the verse as Israel's plea to God to be delivered quickly from exile.
For Rashi, "gazelle" and "fawn" suggest the speed of the anticipated redemption,
while "hill of spices" is a reference to the Temple. Ibn Ezra takes the first words of the
verse as Israel's request that God leave the angels and come down to the "hill of
spices," namely, Mount Zion.

Leviathan

The Leviathan is a primeval sea monster that is mentioned in five places in the Bible
(Isaiah 27:1; Psalms 74:13–14, 104:25–26; Job 3:8, 40:25–41:26). Each context reflects an
ancient battle that took place between God and those who assisted God before the world
was created. The author of each book describes the Leviathan differently. In order to
clarify the Leviathan's role and to make sure that no one saw this monster as an
independent god, the Psalms reports that God created the Leviathan (Psalm 104:25–26).
Later, God would fight this creature, and thus it serves as a symbol of the evil that God
defeats during the time of the ancient Temple. The Rabbis note that following its defeat,
the Leviathan was cut up and saved so that the righteous would be able to gain sustenance from it in the world-to-come.

Drinking Wine Laid down at Creation

According to the Talmud, there are hidden things in this world that only God has
seen. Rabbi Y'hoshua ben Levi tells us that one of these things "is the wine, guarded in

the grape since the six days of Creation." Y'hoshua discerns this through the application of *g'matria* (numerology). The numerical equivalent of *yayin*, "wine," is seventy, the same as *sod*, "secret" (Babylonian Talmud, *B'rachot* 34b).

Gog and Magog

The concept of Gog and Magog as satanic powers that wage war against the righteous at the end of days emerges from a particular understanding of Ezekiel 38–39. According to these verses, "Gog, of the land of Magog, the chief prince of Meshech and Tubal" is to lead an evil army against Israel. As a result of the divine protection of Israel, the Bible goes on to say that these enemies of the Jewish people will be defeated on the mountains of Israel. In the Talmud, the war of Gog and Magog appears frequently in the "messianic wars" that are to precede the coming of the Messiah.

Sheol

While it was never formally described, Sheol appears to have been a well-known notion among the ancient Israelites. Sheol seems to have been understood as a physical place to which one goes down, following this life. Some passages in the Bible indicate that it was thought to be located in the center of the earth (Deuteronomy 32:22; Isaiah 5:14; Proverbs 5:5).

Geihinom

Geihinom, the Jewish version of "hell," literally refers to a valley south of Jerusalem on one of the borders between the territories of Judah and Benjamin (cf. Joshua 15:8, 18:16). During the time of the monarchy, it was a site associated with a cult that burned children, a practice condemned by Jeremiah. In the rabbinic period, the name is used to refer to the place of torment reserved for the wicked after death. It stands in contradistinction to *Gan Eden*, the "Garden of Eden," which, in rabbinic literature, became known as the place of reward for the righteous. In the Bible, these two names never connote the abode of souls after death. Yet, in rabbinic literature, such references abound: in the Babylonian Talmud (*P'sachim* 54a), *Geihinom* and *Gan Eden* existed even before the world was created; *Geihinom* is at the left hand of God and *Gan Eden* at God's right in *Midrash T'hillim* 50:12.

Tribes of Israel

"Tribes of Israel" is a reference to the biblical notion that the descendants of the twelve sons of Jacob formed into twelve tribes or extended family units/clans. Applying the tools of anthropology, some modern scholars contend that the scheme is an artificial one, since the Bible notes other tribal groups, such as the Arameans (Genesis 22:21–24) and the Ishmaelites (Genesis 25:13–16). In addition, in order to maintain the number at twelve, since Levi does not receive a portion of the Land, the tribe of Joseph is divided into Ephraim and Manasseh. While some of the tribes are designated as lineage groups, others are noted for their common geographic background. For the most part, before the tribes were united under David, they acted together only when there was a need to do so. Shortly following Solomon's death, after Simeon had already been integrated into Judah, ten tribes seceded to form the Northern Kingdom (ca. 930 B.C.E.), leaving only Judah and Benjamin in the south.

Rehoboam

As the only son of Solomon, Rehoboam succeeded his father on the throne in Jerusalem. He reigned for seventeen years (975–958 B.C.E.). While he was immediately recognized as the legitimate heir to the throne, there were strong outcries for changes in government. The people felt burdened by the taxes levied upon them by Solomon. However, the people considered Rehoboam's response to be haughty (I Kings 12:14), and he was unable to assuage them. Only the tribe of Judah—joined by the tribe of Benjamin—remained faithful to Rehoboam. The other tribes separated into the Northern Kingdom with Jeroboam as their king. The Northern Kingdom survived until 722 B.C.E., when it was brought down by the Assyrians. During the fifth year of Rehoboam's reign, Jerusalem was attacked by Shisak, one of the kings of Egypt, who was probably stirred into action by Jeroboam. The kingdom continued to deteriorate until it was destroyed by Babylon in 586 B.C.E.

Jeroboam son of Nebat

According to I Kings 11:26–39, Jeroboam was the first king of the ten tribes, reigning for twenty-two years (976–945 B.C.E.). He was the son of the "widow of Zeruah" and worked under Solomon as the chief superintendent of the bands of forced laborers. He worked under the influence of Ahijah. After conspiring to become king of one of the ten tribes, he fled to Egypt (I Kings 11:29–40). Following Solomon's death, the ten tribes invited Jeroboam to become their king. He built up the Northern Kingdom, named Shechem as its capital, and erected "golden calves" at altars in Dan and Bethel in an effort to solidify the divide between the two kingdoms.

Ahijah of Shiloh

Ahijah is identified as a prophet in various places (e.g., I Kings 11:29, 12:15; II Chronicles 9:29, 10:15). He was a younger contemporary of Samuel and Nathan and a member of the so-called association of prophets in or near Shiloh.

United Kingdom

The term "united kingdom" is used to describe the union of the tribes under the government of David. The united kingdom was dissolved shortly after the death of Solomon, when the people rebelled against Rehoboam and the tax burden that Solomon had levied against them.

GLEANINGS

The Mystical Nature of Love

Jewish mystics characteristically play with the numerical equivalent of the Hebrew alphabet to reveal its deeper truths, known as *g'matria*. The Hebrew word for "love," *ahavah*, numerically adds up to thirteen. Twice thirteen is twenty-six, which is numerically equivalent to the term *Adonai*, "God." When two honor the Image of the Divine within each other, there God resides.

Harold Schulweis, Finding Each Other in Judaism: Meditations on the Rites of Passage from Birth to Immortality (New York: UAHC Press, 2001), 44

Our Relationship to God

Some mitzvot obviously concern our direct relationship with God. The precepts surrounding worship and respect for God's name serve as examples. These types of injunctions are known as *mitzvot bein adam lamakom,* commandments between human beings and God. Other precepts serve to regulate our dealings with other people. The Rabbis refer to these as *mitzvot bein adam l'chaveiro,* commandments between a person and his [or her] fellow. But even this latter category comes beneath the aegis of divine concern, for Judaism considers God a partner in each business deal and every marriage. On the High Holy Days, when doing penance for a sin in the category "between a person and his fellow," one must first make restitution and peace with the wronged party. But then one must turn to God for forgiveness as well.

Benjamin Levy, A Faithful Heart: Preparing for the High Holy Days
(New York: UAHC Press, 2001), 14

The Enchantment of Life

In this concluding song [Song 18, 8:13–14], the lover requests the bride to sing a song to him in the hearing of his friends. The bride complies with the request, and sings words which the poet may have meant as his own parting words.

These words the poet had used before in slightly altered form. It was in Song 6, 2:17, that he made the bride dismiss her lover with the same formula. There the bride bids her lover depart until the coming of evening, that in the meantime he may, like the gazelle or young hart, luxuriate among the aromatic perfumes of the mountains, or...revel in love's sweet dreams.

May it not be that in closing his book on a similar note, the poet meant to voice the sentiment, that in the pursuit of love, in its dreams and anticipations, perhaps even more than in the possession of it, lies the enchantment of life?

Israel Bettan, The Five Scrolls: A Commentary (Cincinnati: UAHC Press, 1950), 44–45

Spiritual Intimacy

We are socialized not to share our spiritual lives and beliefs even with those with whom we are most intimate; in fact, most of us lack the language and tools to express the hows and whys of our spiritual feelings and practices. Many of us were raised to believe that only religious professionals and fanatics, or those out to proselytize, speak openly and frequently about religion and the soul. It is not uncommon...[that couples] after five, ten, fifteen years, are just learning about each other's spiritual practices and beliefs. It may be that one partner says a brief prayer every night before going to sleep or before getting on a plane. Or that he feels strongly attached to a particular religious practice or belief. Or that she ascribes importance or meaning to a particular action or ethic. Or that he understands the world in a particular way. Rarely do couples talk seriously and in depth about their beliefs, their reasons for engaging in religious or spiritual practices and rituals, and their connections with the religious or ethnic or national aspects of their identities. This is as true for couples who go to synagogue every Shabbat as it is for those who rarely or never go. Couples do not take the time to wrestle with and share their approaches to questions about their belief in God, their understandings about the meaning of life and death, or the place of spirituality in their lives.

Allowing another person to know about your spiritual life is a profound sign of trust and intimacy. To embark on a life journey with someone, not knowing how they find meaning in the world and in their own existence, can lead to unexpected conflicts, struggles, and confusions.

Daniel Judson and Nancy H. Wiener, Meeting at the Well:
A Jewish Spiritual Guide to Being Engaged (New York: UAHC Press, 2002), 124–25

A Dance Infused with Love

The Song of Songs, little known to many Jews who think of the tradition as prudish and puritanical, is one of the great erotic love poems in all world literature....

In the text of the Song, God is never named; indeed, this is one of only two biblical books in which that is true. Rather than accept the song as a hymn to sensuous joy, the rabbinic tradition reinterpreted the text so as to understand the song allegorically, as a poem about love between God and the People Israel.

But many of today's communities of Jewish renewal have understood the Song in a new way. To them, and clearly to [Marcia] Falk and the Blochs [Chana and Ariel, both of whom have new translations of the text], it is understood as a profoundly spiritual poem not only because it is so drenched in sensuous love of musky fruit and breasts and bellies, the pleasures of the Garden of Eden for grown-ups, but because the fluidity and flow of the poetry evokes a kind of fluid spiritual path that is very different from the "official" path of Rabbinic Judaism. Whereas the Talmud begins, "From what time can we recite the evening *Sh'ma?*" the Song dances with a recurrent refrain: "Never waken love till it is ripe!"

The pleasure of the Song is not an empty physical completion, but a dance infused with love. Yet the Song is not focused on the structures and strictures of marriage. It emerges from a sense that one might call, "There is a time for fluid love, and a time for focused marriage." So the Song—any passage of it that new lovers might choose . . . could act as the central element of a ceremony to make the beginning of a first sexual relationship, a first step on the path to sexual adulthood. . . .

Today we can choose to understand that any task that we perform as sacred, with reverence for the Breath of Life that shapes all work and restfulness, is a way of serving YHWH in the Tent of the Presence. To begin any work with this intention is a potentially sacred act. So we can gather friends and family around the one who is taking this step. They can lean their hands upon his head and give offerings of *tz'daka* (money or actions of social responsibility) to those who need it, and thus make clear the sacred potential of work.

Arthur Ocean Waskow and Phyllis Ocean Berman, *A Time for Every Purpose under Heaven: The Jewish Life-Spiral as a Spiritual Path* (New York: Farrar, Straus and Giroux, 2002), 105–7

Taking the Messiah Seriously

The emancipation of the Jews in the 19th century led to a thorough re-working of the doctrine of the Messiah. The early Reform Jews of Germany made an important change: in the 1841 prayerbook of the Hamburg Temple, the traditional prayers for the coming of the Messiah were replaced by references to a "Messianic age." The early Reformers believed that praying for a King Messiah would hurt their chances for gaining German citizenship. If they were loyal German subjects, how could they justify praying for a Messiah who would re-establish the Jewish state and bring the exiles back to their homeland?

They were also distressed by the miraculous aspect of Messianism. How could a rational person believe that one man, aided by special powers, could single-handedly revolutionize the world order, and inaugurate a time when the dead would be resurrected and judged?

Finally, the Reformers felt that the traditional concept of the Messiah gave human beings too passive roles. Instead of relying on God to redeem the world, they put their faith in enlightened humankind, working together to bring about an era of social justice and universal peace.

The Reformers' dream of a Messianic age was born out of their confidence in human perfectibility, an optimistic conviction that modern science and the spread of democracy would eliminate human misery.

Who takes Messianism seriously today? After the Holocaust and the Gulag, who still believes that education and scientific advancement lead to virtue? After mass murder in Cambodia and genocide in Rwanda, who still believes in the innate goodness of humankind? In an age when hatred and famine and disease still dominate the globe, the sentiments of 19th century liberals sound hollow and naïve....

So what about us? Do we believe in our own power to transform the world? Do we believe that each of us can transform ourselves, that we can be different tomorrow than we were the day before?...

I no longer put my faith in human goodness. Left to ourselves—without moral teaching and religious principles, without the strength and discipline of an ethical community, we are capable of infinite atrocities. But I can't let go of the dream. For deep in my heart, I do believe that we shall overcome the evils of the world...not by our own efforts alone, but with the help of God. God's power, working through us, inspires us to put our minds and hearts and bodies to work in pursuit of the dream.

Janet Marder, "Climbing Jacob's Ladder: Jewish Teachings on the Messiah,"
Sermon Archives, Congregation Beth Am, Los Altos Hills, CA, Dec. 15, 2000, pp. 2–3,
www.betham.org/sermons/marder001215.html.

Bibliography

Alter, Robert. *Genesis: Translation and Commentary.* New York: W.W. Norton & Co., 1996.

Koehler, L. H. and Walter Baumgartner. *Hebrew and Aramaic Lexicon of the Old Testament.* Boston, Mass.: Brill Academic Publishers, 2002.

Biographies

Rabbi Bradley Shavit Artson is the dean of the Ziegler School of Rabbinic Studies, University of Judaism, Los Angeles. He served as rabbi at Congregation Eilat in Mission Viejo, California, and is the author of *It's a Mitzvah! Living Judaism Step-by-Step* and *The Bedside Torah*.

Rabbi Leo Baeck (1873–1956) was a German rabbi and leader of the World Union for Progressive Judaism. Although he was given the right to leave, he chose to stay with his people and eventually survived Theresienstadt. Following World War II, he taught at Hebrew Union College–Jewish Institute of Religion. He is the author of numerous books, including *The Essence of Judaism* and *Judaism and Christianity*.

Phyllis Ocean Berman directs Elat Chayyim's Summer Retreat Program and is coauthor of *Tales of Tikkun*.

Rabbi Israel Bettan (1889–1957) was professor of homiletics at Hebrew Union College–Jewish Institute of Religion, Cincinnati.

Rabbi Terry Bookman is the senior rabbi of Temple Beth Am in Miami, Florida, and the author of two books on Jewish spirituality.

Rabbi Eugene B. Borowitz is the Sigmund L. Falk Distinguished Professor of Education and Jewish Religious Thought at Hebrew Union College–Jewish Institute of Religion, where he has taught since 1962. He is the author of numerous books, including *Renewing the Covenant*, and was the first person to receive a National Foundation for Jewish Culture Achievement Award in Scholarship for work in the field of Jewish thought.

Rabbi Reuven Bulka has been the spiritual leader of Congregation Machzikei Hadas in Ottawa since 1967 and the founding editor of the *Journal of Psychology and Judaism* since 1976. He holds a Ph.D. in logotherapy from the University of Ottawa and is the author/editor of over twenty-five books.

Rabbi Norman Cohen is provost of Hebrew Union College–Jewish Institute of Religion, where he also serves as professor of midrash at its New York campus. He is the author of several books, including *Self, Struggle and Change: Family Conflict Stories in Genesis and Their Healing Insights for Our Lives*.

Rabbi Amy Eilberg is a spiritual counselor in private practice.

Merle Feld is an award-winning playwright and poet whose work has appeared in numerous anthologies and prayer books. Her plays *Across the Jordan* and *The Gates Are Closing* have been read and staged at synagogues and universities across the country and internationally.

Rabbi Michael Gold serves as the spiritual leader of Temple Beth Torah in Tamarac, Florida. He has served congregations in Pittsburgh and in Upper Nyack, New York. Rabbi Gold is the author of *And Hannah Wept, Does God Belong in the Bedroom*, and *God, Love, Sex and Family*.

Rabbi Elyse Goldstein is director of Kolel: A Center for Liberal Jewish Learning, near Toronto, Ontario, and author of *Seek Her Out: A Textual Approach to the Study of Women and Judaism*.

Rabbi Daniel Gordis is the assistant director of the Mandel Foundation in Jerusalem, a program for the training of Jewish educators. Formerly, he taught at the University of Judaism in Los Angeles, where he was also the dean of the rabbinic program. He is the author of two books and numerous articles.

Rabbi Arthur Green is dean of the Rabbinical School at Hebrew College and author of numerous works on Jewish spirituality and mysticism, including *Seek My Face: A Jewish Mystical Theology*.

Joel Lurie Grishaver is the Creative Chairperson of Torah Aura Productions. He is among America's most innovative Jewish educators and the author of numerous books and articles.

Rabbi Daniel Judson is the spiritual leader of Temple Beth David of the South Shore in Canton, Massachusetts. He is the coauthor of *The Rituals and Practices of a Jewish Life: A Handbook for Personal Spiritual Renewal* and *Meeting at the Well: A Jewish Spiritual Guide to Being Engaged*.

Rabbi Lawrence Kushner is the scholar-in-residence at Congregation Emanu-El in San Francisco. Most recently, he was rabbi-in-residence at Hebrew Union College–Jewish Institute of Religion, New York. Rabbi Kushner served as spiritual leader of Congregation Beth El of Sudbury, Massachusetts, for twenty-five years and is the author of numerous books and articles, including *God Was in This Place and I, I Did Not Know*.

Rabbi Shoni Labowitz draws from the various mystical traditions in the development of her spiritual health spa called Living Waters. She hosts the radio program Spiritual Focus and serves as co-rabbi with her husband Phillip Labowitz of Temple Adath Or in Fort Lauderdale, Florida.

Rabbi Benjamin Levy is rabbi of the Monroe Township Jewish Center in Spotswood, New Jersey.

Rabbi Joseph Narot was rabbi of Temple Israel in Miami, Florida.

Dr. Carol Ochs is director of graduate studies at Hebrew Union College–Jewish Institute of Religion, New York, where she is also adjunct associate professor of Jewish religious thought. She is the author of numerous works on spirituality, including *Reaching Godward, Women and Spirituality* and *Our Lives as Torah*, and coauthor of *Jewish Spiritual Guidance*.

Rabbi Sally Priesand is the rabbi of Monmouth Reform Temple in Tinton Falls, New Jersey. She was the first woman to be ordained as a rabbi in the United States.

Melinda Ribner, C.S.W., is the founder and director of The Jewish Meditation Circle and author of *Everyday Kabbalah: A Practical Guide for Meditation, Healing and Personal Growth*.

Rabbi Zalman Schachter-Shalomi is the founder of the Jewish Renewal movement. He was ordained as a Lubavitch-trained rabbi and received a doctorate from Hebrew Union College–Jewish Institute of Religion. He is the author of *Spiritual Intimacy: A Study of Counseling in Hasidism, Fragments of a Future Scroll,* and *The First Step: A Guide for the New Jewish Spirit.*

Rabbi Harold Schulweis is the senior rabbi of Valley Beth Shalom in Encino, California. He is the founder of the Jewish Foundation for Rescuers and the author of *For Those Who Can't Believe* and *Finding Each Other in Judaism.*

Rabbi Arthur Ocean Waskow is a leader in Jewish Renewal movement and director of the Shalom Center.

Frances Weinman Schwartz is a teacher of adult Jewish education and Holocaust studies, author of *Passage to Pesach,* and producer of a monthly book discussion program sponsored by New York Kollel.

Rabbi Harlan J. Wechsler is spiritual leader of Congregation Or Zarua in New York City and visiting assistant professor at the Jewish Theological Seminary of America, where he teaches theology and ethics.

Rabbi Nancy Wiener is the clinical director of the Jacob and Hilda Blaustein Center for Pastoral Counseling at Hebrew Union College–Jewish Institute of Religion in New York, where she is also adjunct associate professor of pastoral care and counseling. She is the author of *Beyond Breaking the Glass: A Spiritual Guide to Your Jewish Wedding* and coauthor of *Meeting at the Well: A Jewish Spiritual Guide to Being Engaged.*